Heroes of the Coffee Rota

To Audrey & the Coffee team.
Hope you'll be back in action soon.
Sign and pass on once you've
had your fill.
                              MaB.

Read by :
MaB,
Audrey G
Brenda H
Helen H
ARLENE H
Muriel
Carol A

Betty E.
Janet Gregory

Also by Dave Walker and available from
Canterbury Press

Peculiar Goings On
The Exciting World of Churchgoing
The Dave Walker Guide to the Church
My Pew: Things I Have Seen from It

www.canterburypress.co.uk

Heroes of the Coffee Rota

Dave Walker

CANTERBURY
PRESS

Norwich

© Dave Walker 2015

First published in 2015 by the Canterbury Press Norwich
Editorial office
3rd Floor, Invicta House,
108–114 Golden Lane,
London EC1Y 0TG

Canterbury Press is an imprint of Hymns Ancient & Modern Ltd
(a registered charity)
13A Hellesdon Park Road, Norwich,
Norfolk, NR6 5DR, UK

www.canterburypress.co.uk

British Library Cataloguing in Publication data

A catalogue record for this book is available
from the British Library

978-1-84825-820-4

Printed and bound in Great Britain by
CPI Group (UK) Ltd

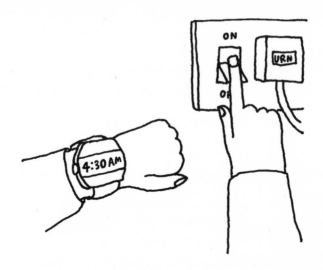

Thanks to everyone who has contributed to this, the fifth volume of my cartoons. In particular my friends and family, those who send me ideas, and those who support and use my work via my CartoonChurch.com website.

This book is for everyone who keeps the church going. Those who lead, arrange, preach, attend, teach, clean, collate or mow something, and many others who you'll find depicted in the ninety diagrams that follow. And, in particular, the heroes of the coffee rota.

Dave Walker
June 2015

GOING BACK TO CHURCH

ADVICE FOR THOSE RETURNING AFTER QUITE SOME TIME

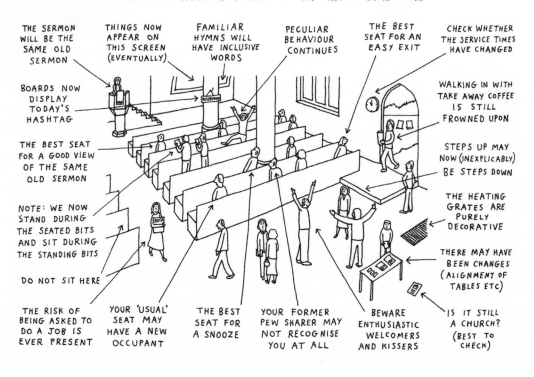

SAVING SEATS

HOW TO DO IT

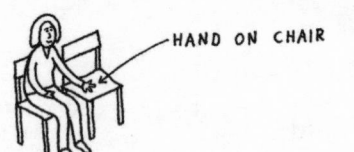

HAND ON CHAIR

ONE SEAT

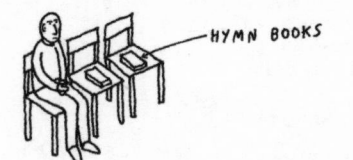

HYMN BOOKS

TWO SEATS

A FEW COATS

A ROW

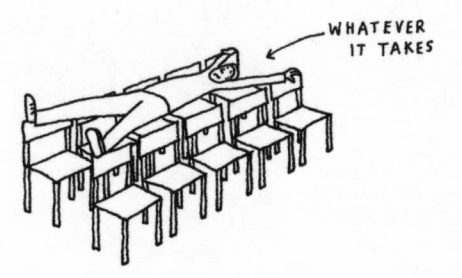

WHATEVER IT TAKES

SEVERAL ROWS

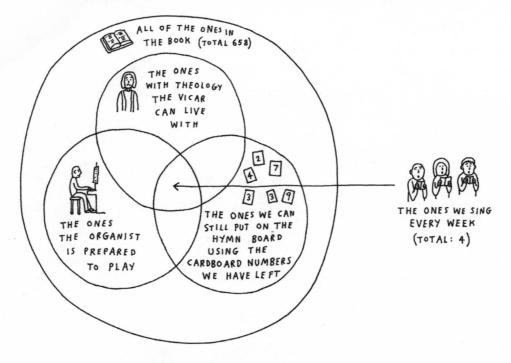

CHOOSING THE HYMNS

ALL OF THE ONES IN THE BOOK (TOTAL 658)

THE ONES WITH THEOLOGY THE VICAR CAN LIVE WITH

THE ONES THE ORGANIST IS PREPARED TO PLAY

THE ONES WE CAN STILL PUT ON THE HYMN BOARD USING THE CARDBOARD NUMBERS WE HAVE LEFT

2 4 7 3 3 9

THE ONES WE SING EVERY WEEK (TOTAL: 4)

READING THE LESSON

ADVICE

SPEND TIME REHEARSING
AT HOME

WORK ON YOUR DICTION
AT EVERY OPPORTUNITY

TURN UP

ADJUST THE MICROPHONE
AND LECTERN LIGHT

THIS IS THE
WORD OF
THE LORD

TRY NOT TO RUSH

BE CONFIDENT—
RELAX AND ENJOY IT

THE LECTIONARY

THE PERILS OF DEPARTING FROM IT

A SPECIAL
MICROPHONE
WILL
DETECT
THE
ANOMALY

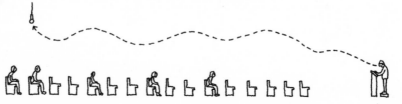

THE
INFORMATION
IS BEAMED
TO THE
ARCHBISHOP'S
PALACE

IN THE
THRONE
ROOM
A SCREEN
SHOWS
THIS
WEEK'S
TRANSGRESSIONS

FORTUNATELY THE ARCHBISHOP IS TERRIBLY
BUSY WITH SERMON PREPARATION, ETC

YOU WILL PROBABLY GET AWAY
WITH A FIXED PENALTY

THE INTERCESSIONS

HOW TO PREPARE THEM

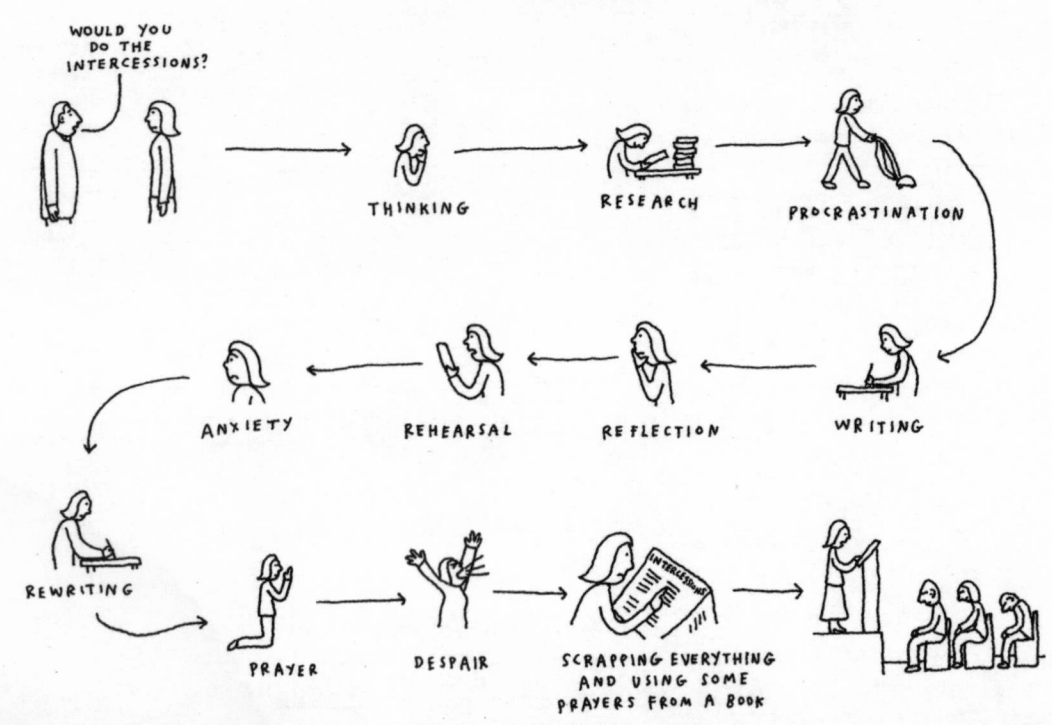

THE COLLECTION PLATE

REASONS TO LET IT PASS

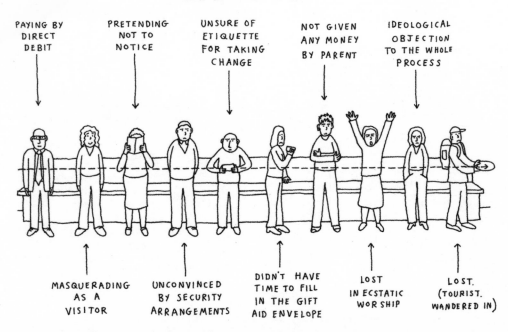

THE NOTICES

CONVEY THE INFORMATION BY A VARIETY OF MEANS TO MAKE SURE IT GETS THROUGH

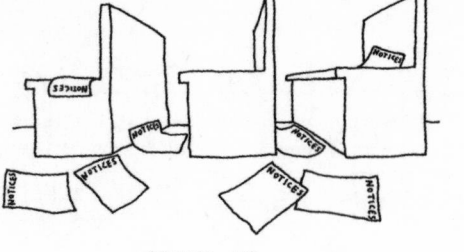

PRINT IT

READ IT OUT

PUT IT ON A GIANT SCREEN

POST IT ON THE WEBSITE

HOW TO ESCAPE

WHEN YOU DISCOVER THAT IT IS 'ALL AGE' SUNDAY

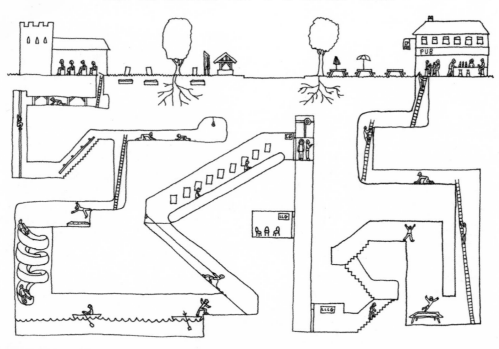

DIFFERENT AGES

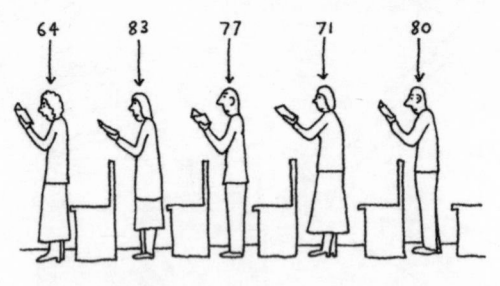

AT THE BEGINNING OF THE SERVICE
WE ALL JOIN IN TOGETHER

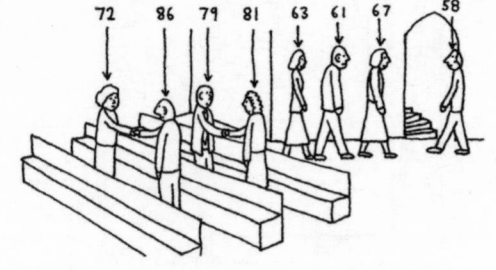

DURING THE PEACE THE YOUNGER ONES
GO OUT TO THEIR GROUPS

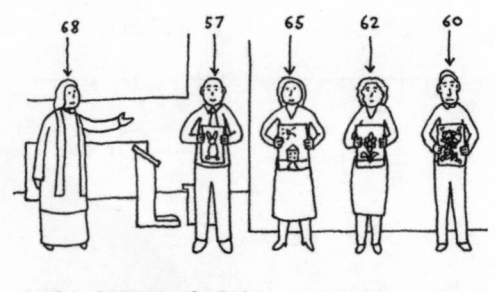

THEY RETURN BEFORE COMMUNION, AND
SHOW US THE WORK THEY HAVE DONE

ONE SUNDAY EACH MONTH WE GATHER
FOR AN 'ALL-AGE' SERVICE

THE COMBINED SUNDAY SCHOOL

FOR CHURCHES WITHOUT SUNDAY SCHOOL TEACHERS

THE CHILDREN'S TALK

PITFALLS TO AVOID

APPEARING UNEXPECTEDLY
WEARING A SCARY OUTFIT

ASKING QUESTIONS WITHOUT
REQUIRING A HAND IN THE AIR

PRE-EMPTING ALL THREE
POINTS OF THE VICAR'S SERMON

RUNNING OUT OF SWEETS

ASKING A QUESTION WHERE
THE ANSWER ISN'T JESUS

SAYING ANYTHING AT ALL
ABOUT FATHER CHRISTMAS

THE SUNDAY SCHOOL

PROJECTS THAT PROVED, IN HINDSIGHT, TO BE RATHER OVERAMBITIOUS
GIVEN THE HOUR-LONG DURATION OF THE MORNING SERVICE

A LIFESIZE RECONSTRUCTION
OF NOAH'S ARK

ACTING OUT THE BOOK
OF REVELATION

LEARNING PSALM 119
OFF BY HEART

PERFECTING TALLIS'S
'SPEM IN ALIUM'

CHILDREN'S CRAFT ITEMS

WHAT HAPPENS TO THEM

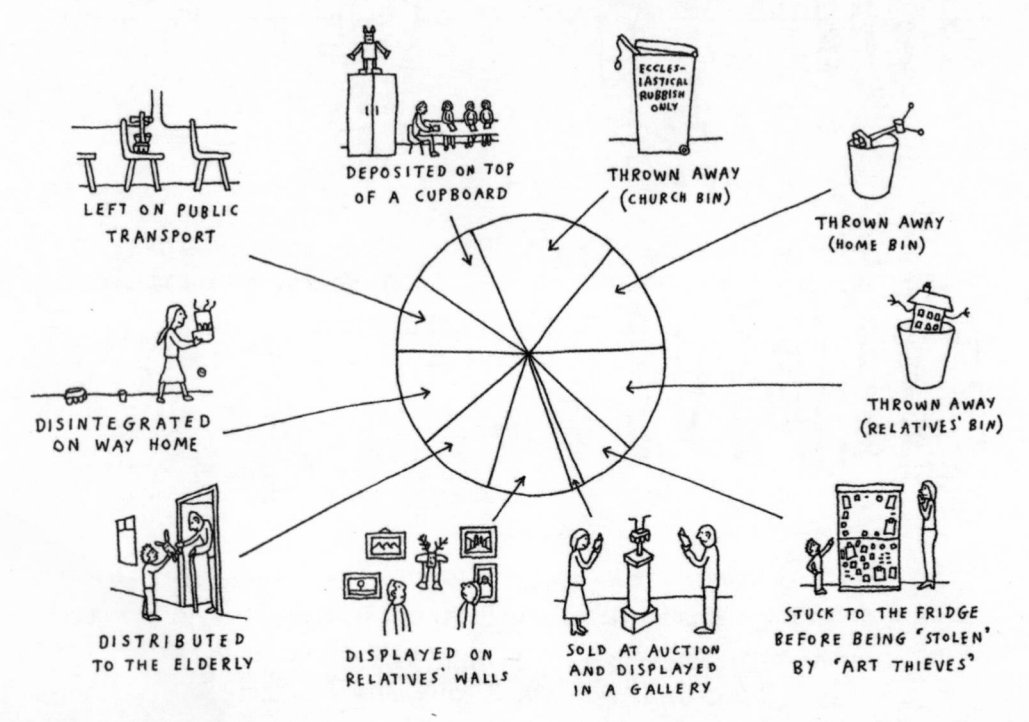

YOUNG PEOPLE

HOW TO STOP THEM LEAVING THE CHURCH

GET THEM INVOLVED

LET THEM LEAD THE SERVICE

ENCOURAGE THE CONGREGATION
TO BE MORE YOUTH-FRIENDLY

ADJUST THE SERVICE TIME

SEND THEM ON A
LIFE-CHANGING TRIP

LOCK THE DOORS

DONATIONS

WE NEED THE FOLLOWING THINGS FOR THE YOUTH WORK

FOOD THAT IS NOT FAR OFF BEING WITHIN DATE

TECHNOLOGY FROM RECENT DECADES

JIGSAW PICTURES THAT MAY OR MAY NOT BE COMPLETE

SPORTS EQUIPMENT FROM THE 1970s

PARAPHERNALIA FROM COMPETING RELIGIONS

MILITARY EQUIPMENT

RECRUITING VOLUNTEERS

TEN APPROACHES

ROTAS

HOW TO COPE IF YOU ARE ALLOCATED MORE THAN ONE DUTY

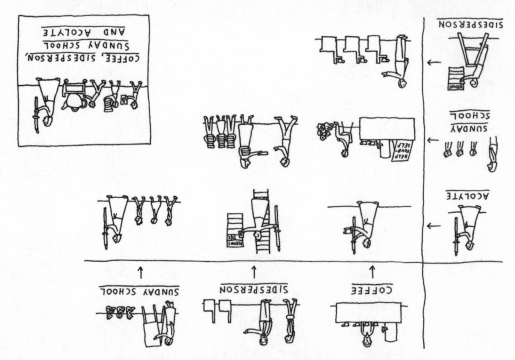

THE NATIONAL FLOWER ROTA

THE TEA ROTA

INSTRUCTIONS FOR MAKING AFTER-CHURCH TEA

① ARRIVE 7 HOURS BEFOREHAND
TO PUT THE URN ON

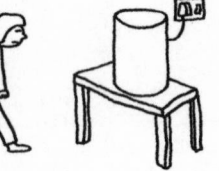

② PUT ONE TEABAG INTO THE
LARGE TEAPOT, AND FILL WITH WATER

③ FILL EACH PLASTIC DISPOSABLE CUP
HALF FULL OF MILK, THEN POUR TEA

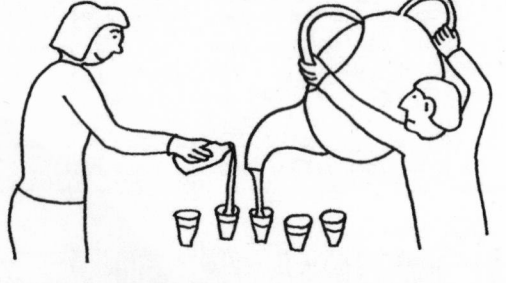

④ AFTERWARDS, WASH UP THE
PLASTIC DISPOSABLE CUPS
FOR USE NEXT SUNDAY

WHO DOES THEM?

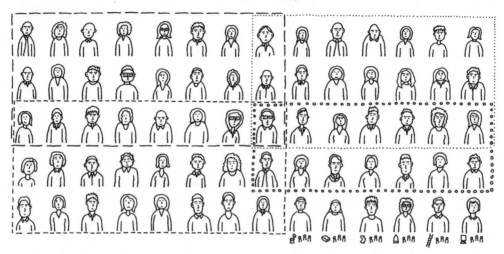

THE JOBS THAT NEED DOING

- CLEANING THE TOILETS
- WASHING THE TEA TOWELS
- DUSTING THE WINDOW LEDGES
- CLIMBING THE LADDER TO CLEAR THE GUTTERS
- GOING TO COMMITTEE MEETINGS
- GIVING OUT HYMN BOOKS
- MAKING THE CHURCH OFFICE COMPUTER WORK
- CHANGING THE STAGNANT PREACHER'S WATER

REASONS FOR INACTIVITY

- —— TOO BUSY
- ----- TOO IMPORTANT
- .... MANAGED TO GET OUT OF IT THUS FAR
- ○○○○○ INCOMPETENT

SIDESPERSONS

TYPICAL OFF-DUTY ACTIVITIES

GIVING OUT HYMN BOOKS

DIRECTING PEOPLE TO SEATS

PASSING AROUND A COLLECTION PLATE

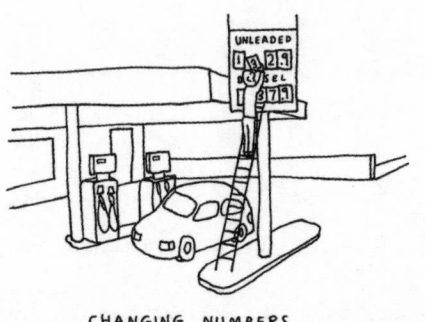

CHANGING NUMBERS

ACOLYTE TRAINING

TOPICS COVERED

GETTING INTO AN ALB

FIRE SAFETY

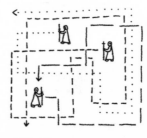

STAGE MANAGEMENT

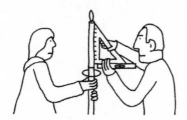

MAINTAINING
PERPENDICULARITY

KNOWING WHEN TO STAND
STILL AND WHEN TO WALK

WHAT TO DO IF YOUR
FLAME GOES OUT

JOINING THE CHOIR

YOU WILL NEED A ROBE

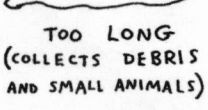

TOO LONG
(COLLECTS DEBRIS
AND SMALL ANIMALS)

TOO SHORT
(KNEES VISIBLE)

YOU WILL NEED TO MULTITASK
IE WALK AND SING SIMULTANEOUSLY

IF YOU FIND THIS DIFFICULT PRACTICE
OTHER FORMS OF MULTITASKING, EG:

READING
A BOOK
WHILST
PLAYING
TENNIS

SURFING THE
INTERNET
WHILST
CLEANING
OUT THE
GUTTERING

THE CHOIR

MINOR MISDEMEANOURS TAKING PLACE IN YOUR SUNDAY SERVICES

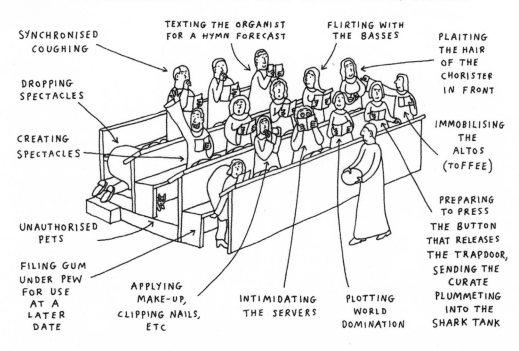

SYNCHRONISED COUGHING

TEXTING THE ORGANIST FOR A HYMN FORECAST

FLIRTING WITH THE BASSES

PLAITING THE HAIR OF THE CHORISTER IN FRONT

DROPPING SPECTACLES

CREATING SPECTACLES

IMMOBILISING THE ALTOS (TOFFEE)

UNAUTHORISED PETS

FILING GUM UNDER PEW FOR USE AT A LATER DATE

APPLYING MAKE-UP, CLIPPING NAILS, ETC

INTIMIDATING THE SERVERS

PLOTTING WORLD DOMINATION

PREPARING TO PRESS THE BUTTON THAT RELEASES THE TRAPDOOR, SENDING THE CURATE PLUMMETING INTO THE SHARK TANK

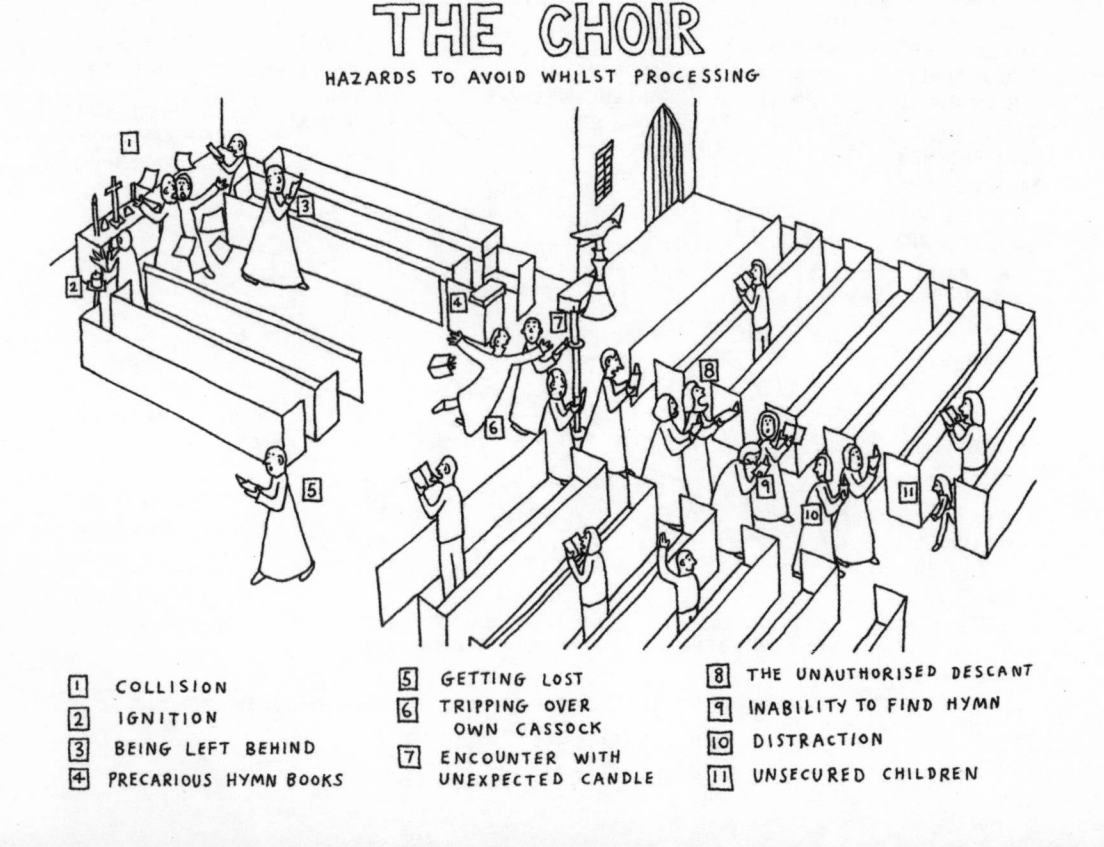

THE CHOIR

HAZARDS TO AVOID WHILST PROCESSING

1. COLLISION
2. IGNITION
3. BEING LEFT BEHIND
4. PRECARIOUS HYMN BOOKS
5. GETTING LOST
6. TRIPPING OVER OWN CASSOCK
7. ENCOUNTER WITH UNEXPECTED CANDLE
8. THE UNAUTHORISED DESCANT
9. INABILITY TO FIND HYMN
10. DISTRACTION
11. UNSECURED CHILDREN

THE MUSIC GROUP

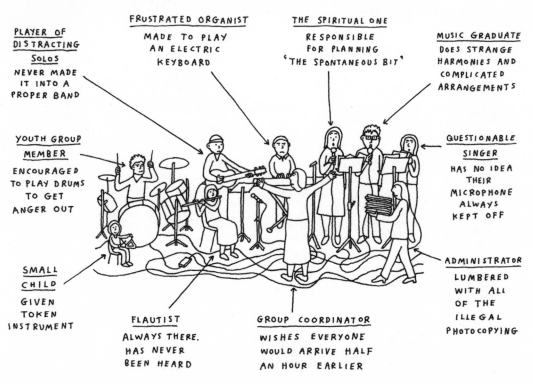

PLAYER OF DISTRACTING SOLOS
NEVER MADE IT INTO A PROPER BAND

FRUSTRATED ORGANIST
MADE TO PLAY AN ELECTRIC KEYBOARD

THE SPIRITUAL ONE
RESPONSIBLE FOR PLANNING 'THE SPONTANEOUS BIT'

MUSIC GRADUATE
DOES STRANGE HARMONIES AND COMPLICATED ARRANGEMENTS

YOUTH GROUP MEMBER
ENCOURAGED TO PLAY DRUMS TO GET ANGER OUT

QUESTIONABLE SINGER
HAS NO IDEA THEIR MICROPHONE ALWAYS KEPT OFF

SMALL CHILD
GIVEN TOKEN INSTRUMENT

FLAUTIST
ALWAYS THERE. HAS NEVER BEEN HEARD

GROUP COORDINATOR
WISHES EVERYONE WOULD ARRIVE HALF AN HOUR EARLIER

ADMINISTRATOR
LUMBERED WITH ALL OF THE ILLEGAL PHOTOCOPYING

THE SMALL GROUP

TAKING DRINKS ORDERS — THE INTERNATIONALLY-RECOGNISED SIGNALS

TEA   COFFEE   STRONG   WEAK   MILKY

NUMBERS OF SUGARS   NO MILK   SQUASH   POP   GIN

THE ELECTORAL ROLL

REASONS TO JOIN IT

① YOU WILL DECIDE WHO SHOULD BE ON THE P.C.C. AND DEANERY SYNOD

CHOOSE THREE CANDIDATES

② YOU CAN PLAY A FULL PART IN THE LIFE OF THE CHURCH

CHURCH MEMBERS PLEASE SIGN UP FOR JOBS HERE

SUNDAY SCHOOL · DOING THE SOUND SYSTEM · CLEANING · YOUTH · TEA · FLOWERS

③ IT WILL BOOST THE MORALE OF THE CLERGY

NUMBERS UP

④ THERE MAY BE A THANK YOU PRESENT — SEASIDE CONFECTIONARY PERHAPS

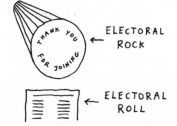

THANK YOU FOR JOINING

← ELECTORAL ROCK

← ELECTORAL ROLL

⑤ YOUR NAME WILL BE EXHIBITED IN CHURCH FOR 14 DAYS

THE P.C.C. MEETING

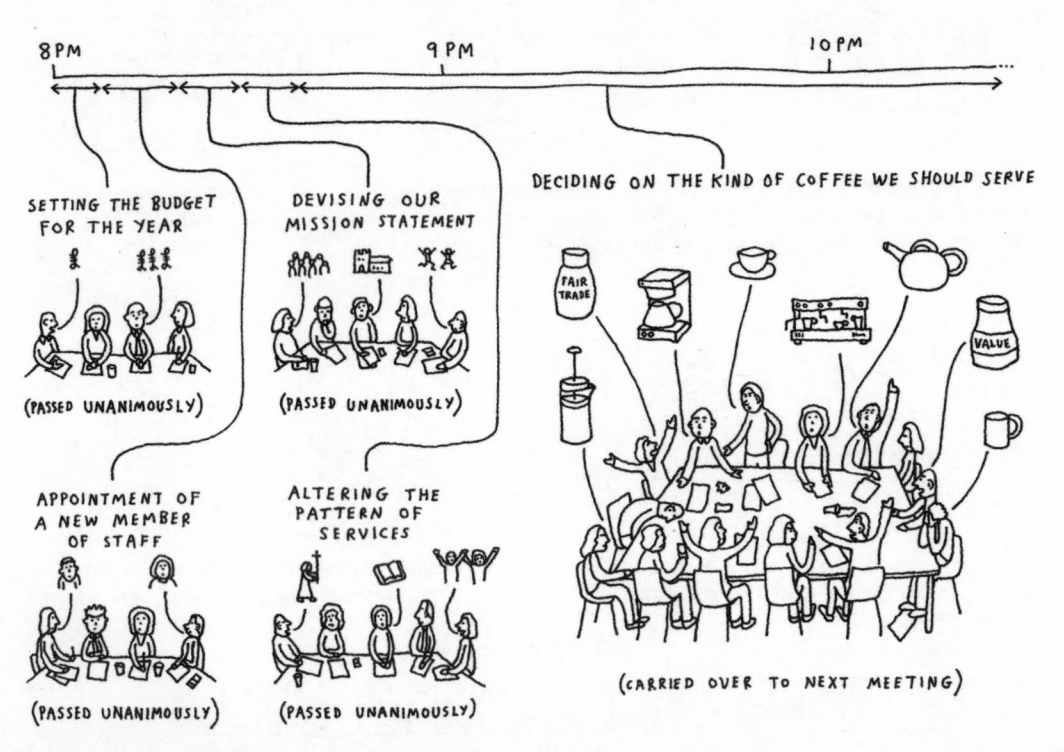

8 PM

9 PM

10 PM

...

SETTING THE BUDGET FOR THE YEAR

(PASSED UNANIMOUSLY)

DEVISING OUR MISSION STATEMENT

(PASSED UNANIMOUSLY)

DECIDING ON THE KIND OF COFFEE WE SHOULD SERVE

FAIR TRADE

VALUE

APPOINTMENT OF A NEW MEMBER OF STAFF

(PASSED UNANIMOUSLY)

ALTERING THE PATTERN OF SERVICES

(PASSED UNANIMOUSLY)

(CARRIED OVER TO NEXT MEETING)

THE P.C.C SURVIVAL KIT

(FILE CONTAINING SECRET COMPARTMENTS FOR PAROCHIAL CHURCH COUNCIL ESSENTIALS)

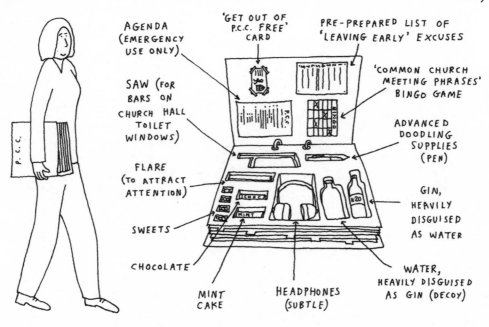

P.C.C. BINGO

WORDS AND PHRASES OFTEN USED DURING MEETINGS
OF THE PAROCHIAL CHURCH COUNCIL

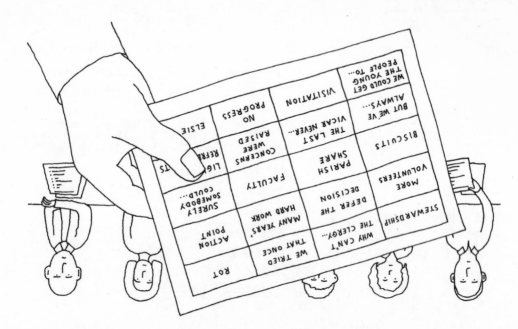

THE DEANERY SYNOD REP.

HOW TO AVOID VOLUNTEERING TO FILL THE VACANCY

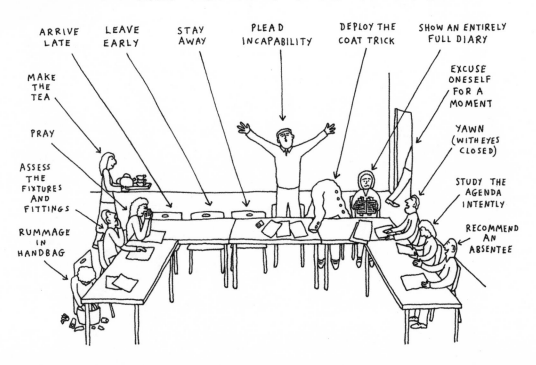

ARRIVE LATE

LEAVE EARLY

STAY AWAY

PLEAD INCAPABILITY

DEPLOY THE COAT TRICK

SHOW AN ENTIRELY FULL DIARY

MAKE THE TEA

PRAY

EXCUSE ONESELF FOR A MOMENT

ASSESS THE FIXTURES AND FITTINGS

YAWN (WITH EYES CLOSED)

RUMMAGE IN HANDBAG

STUDY THE AGENDA INTENTLY

RECOMMEND AN ABSENTEE

CHANGES

WAYS TO RESIST THEM

OBJECT
AT A MEETING

START
A PETITION

CALL
THE BISHOP

USE
SOCIAL MEDIA

TAKE
DIRECT ACTION

HIDE
THE PLANS

GET
IN THE WAY

BRIBE
SOMEONE TO KEEP
THINGS AS THEY ARE

SING
A PROTEST SONG

CARRY OUT
LATE NIGHT SABOTAGE

PICKET
THE CHURCH

BOYCOTT
SUNDAY SERVICES

THREATEN
TO PAY COLLECTION
IN SMALL CHANGE

RAISE
FEAR AND ALARM

WRITE
IN THE PARISH
MAGAZINE

SUNDAY MORNING

WE ARE DWINDLING

THE KIDS ARE PLAYING FOOTBALL
FED UP WITH CHURCH POLITICS
FOUND LAST WEEK'S SERMON UNCOMFORTABLE
OVERSLEPT
LATE NIGHT LAST NIGHT
NO ONE HERE TALKS TO ME
THE CHILDREN WON'T KEEP QUIET, AND PEOPLE STARE
SITTING IN THE COFFEE SHOP, READING THE PAPER
THE THURSDAY NIGHT HOME GROUP IS MY CHURCH
IN TROUBLE IF I DON'T BUILD THAT WARDROBE

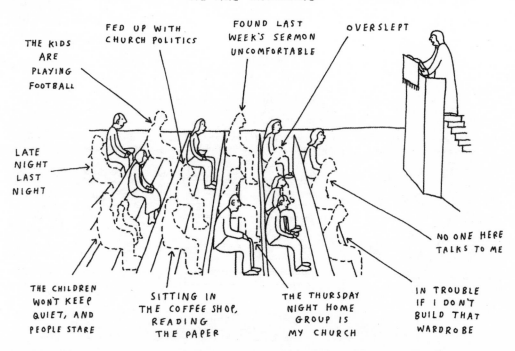

THE COMBINED SERVICE

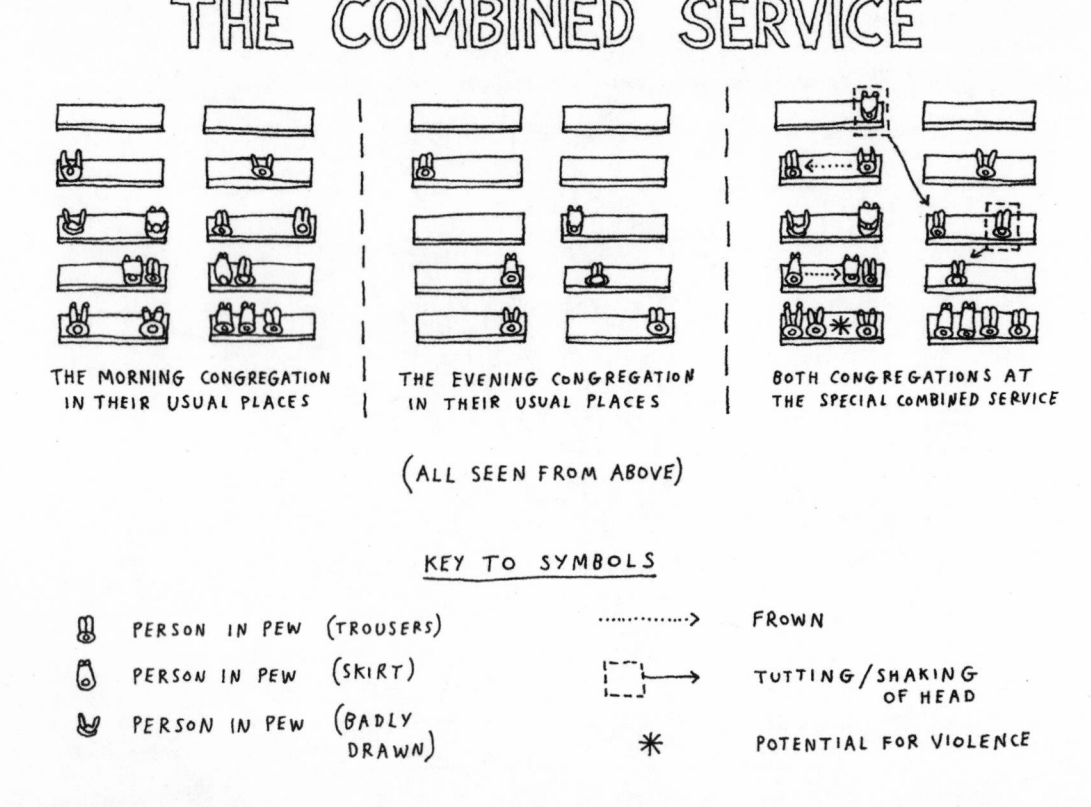

THE MORNING CONGREGATION IN THEIR USUAL PLACES

THE EVENING CONGREGATION IN THEIR USUAL PLACES

BOTH CONGREGATIONS AT THE SPECIAL COMBINED SERVICE

(ALL SEEN FROM ABOVE)

KEY TO SYMBOLS

PERSON IN PEW (TROUSERS)

PERSON IN PEW (SKIRT)

PERSON IN PEW (BADLY DRAWN)

⋯⋯⋯> FROWN

TUTTING/SHAKING OF HEAD

* POTENTIAL FOR VIOLENCE

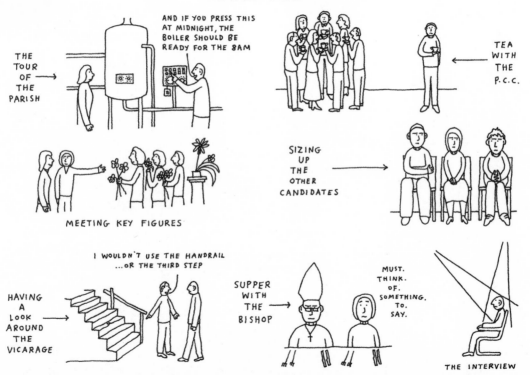

INTERVIEWING

FOR A NEW VICAR

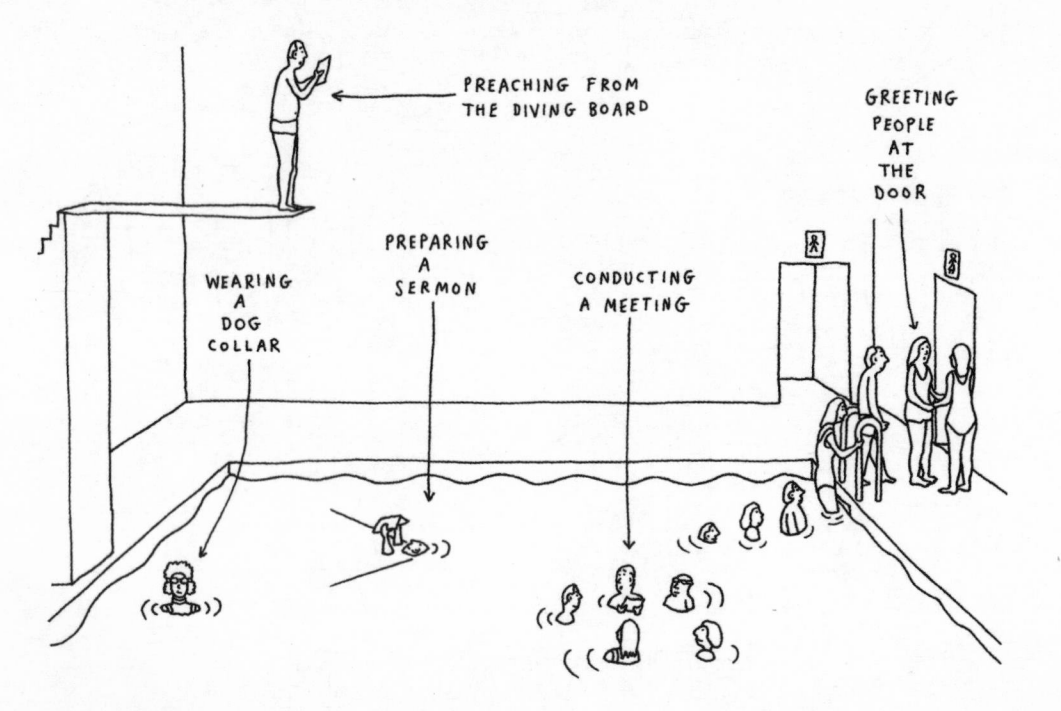

CLERGY

HOW TO RECOGNISE THEM IN THE SWIMMING POOL

PREACHING FROM
THE DIVING BOARD

GREETING
PEOPLE
AT
THE
DOOR

PREPARING
A
SERMON

WEARING
A
DOG
COLLAR

CONDUCTING
A MEETING

CLERGY DEPLOYMENT

THE BISHOPS DECIDE WHO GOES WHERE

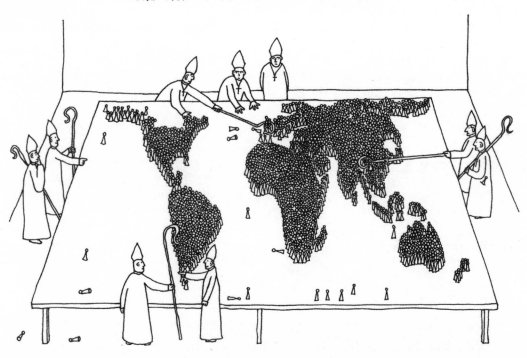

THE CLERGY CONFERENCE

① IS IT COFFEE BREAK SOON?
② I COULD HAVE BEEN AN ASTRONAUT
③ IT IS SO COLD IN HERE
④ HOPE THE CATS ARE OK
⑤ WISH HE'D SNORE QUIETLY
⑥ HOW RUDE!
⑦ OH NO - HE'S MY ROOM MATE
⑧ OOH - FACEBOOK MESSAGE!
⑨ IT IS SO HOT IN HERE

⑩ WHAT TIME SHALL I PHONE?
⑪ SO MUCH TO DO WHEN I RETURN
⑫ WHICH PUB SHALL WE GO TO?
⑬ I'M TWEETING THIS
⑭ ZZ ZZ
⑮ HE MIGHT MISS SOMETHING
⑯ HOW VERY EMBARRASSING
⑰ WHY AM I HERE AGAIN?
⑱ LOOK AT THOSE FIELDS

⑲ CAN WE GET BACK TO THE TEXT?
⑳ WONDER WHAT'S FOR DINNER
㉑ ISN'T ⑮ LOVELY?
㉒ SERMON ILLUSTRATION!
㉓ OH DEAR - DRIBBLE
㉔ WHEN I'M BISHOP ALL THIS WILL BE MINE
㉕ WOULDN'T MIND HIS PARISH
㉖ ....

DAYS OFF

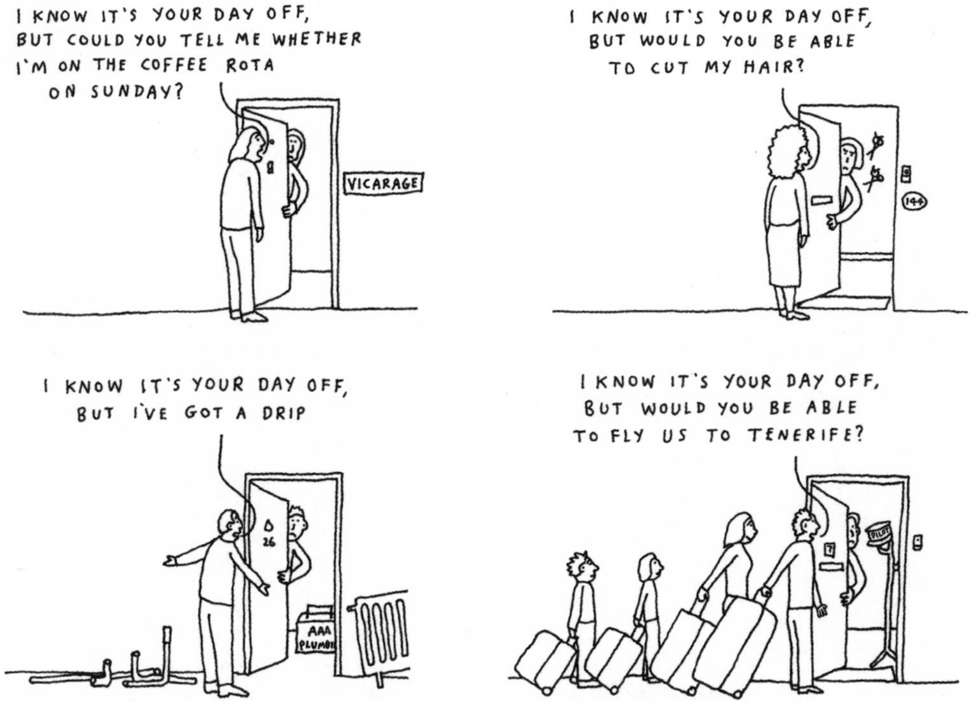
I KNOW IT'S YOUR DAY OFF, BUT COULD YOU TELL ME WHETHER I'M ON THE COFFEE ROTA ON SUNDAY?
VICARAGE
I KNOW IT'S YOUR DAY OFF, BUT WOULD YOU BE ABLE TO CUT MY HAIR?
144
I KNOW IT'S YOUR DAY OFF, BUT I'VE GOT A DRIP
26
AAA
I KNOW IT'S YOUR DAY OFF, BUT WOULD YOU BE ABLE TO FLY US TO TENERIFE?
PILOT

THE VICAR'S BREAK

HOW WE ARE GOING TO COPE

BETTY WILL
SET UP THE
MICROPHONES

KEVIN WILL
BOX THE
BAUBLES

ARTHUR WILL
TURN ON
THE HEATING

GLADYS WILL
FOLD THE
SERVICE SHEETS

BRIAN WILL WAIT IN
CHURCH FOR THE LADY
TRACING HER ANCESTORS

ROSEMARY WILL OPEN
AND BIN THE
CHURCH-FURNISHINGS
CATALOGUES

DAVID WILL PUT
THE CHAIRS BACK
IN A SYMMETRICAL
PATTERN

TINA WILL SCRAPE
THE CANDLE WAX OFF
THE WINDOW LEDGES
USING THE (EXPIRED)
PARISH CREDIT CARD

SUSAN WILL
CATEGORISE THE
LOST UMBRELLAS

NIGEL WILL
TAKE CHARGE
OF THE GRIT

TAKING TIME OFF

ADVICE FOR CLERGY: HOW TO STAY AT HOME DURING A WEEK OFF WITHOUT BEING DETECTED

WEAR A DISGUISE

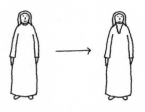

BEFORE　　　　AFTER

RETIRE TO THE CELLAR

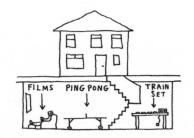

FILMS　PING PONG　TRAIN SET

DEVELOP A MILK STRATEGY

ORDER TWICE AS MANY AS USUAL

TAKE IN HALF. LEAVE HALF ON THE DOORSTEP

PUT THE LIGHTS ON TIMERS

BUT NOT THE CURTAINS

USE THE SECRET PASSAGE

OPEN IT BY PUSHING THIS STATUE

OR THIS BOOK

OR PERHAPS THIS PANEL

MOVE SUBTLY AROUND THE VICARAGE

THE NEW CURATE

MEMBERS OF THE PAROCHIAL CHURCH COUNCIL WILL VISIT, ON A ROTA BASIS, BEARING GIFTS

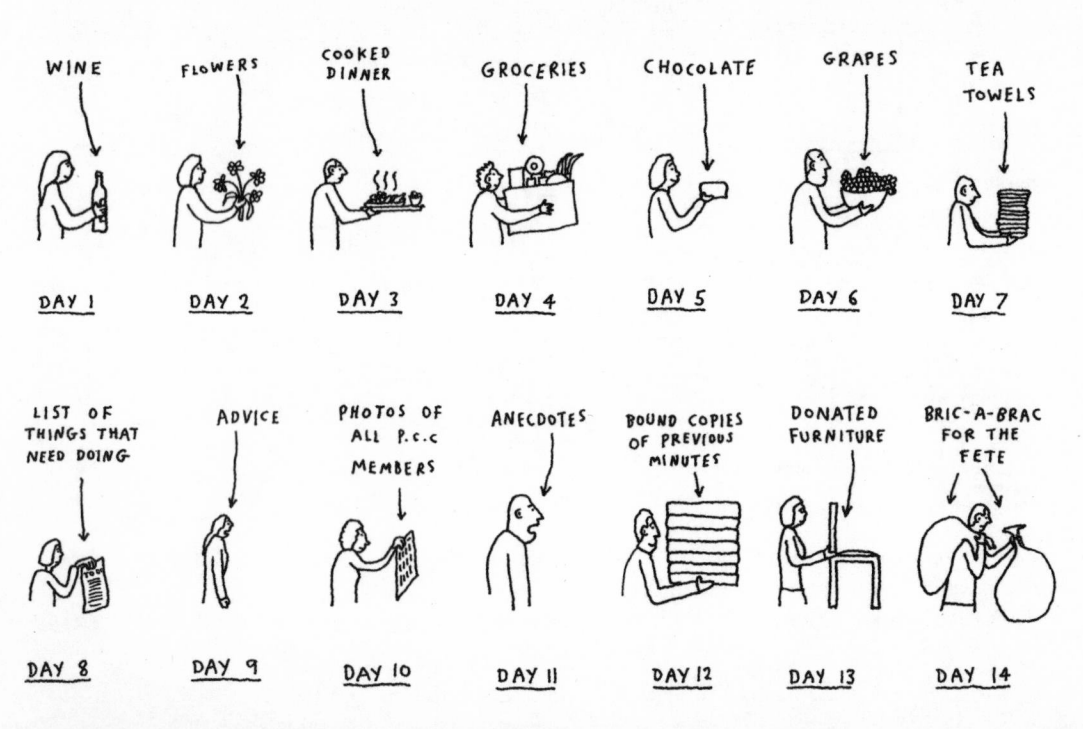

THE BEETLE DRIVE

CURATE EDITION

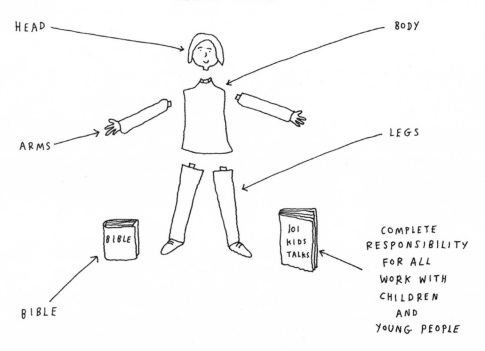

HEAD

BODY

ARMS

LEGS

BIBLE

101 KIDS TALKS

COMPLETE
RESPONSIBILITY
FOR ALL
WORK WITH
CHILDREN
AND
YOUNG PEOPLE

CURATES

HOW USEFUL ARE THEY?

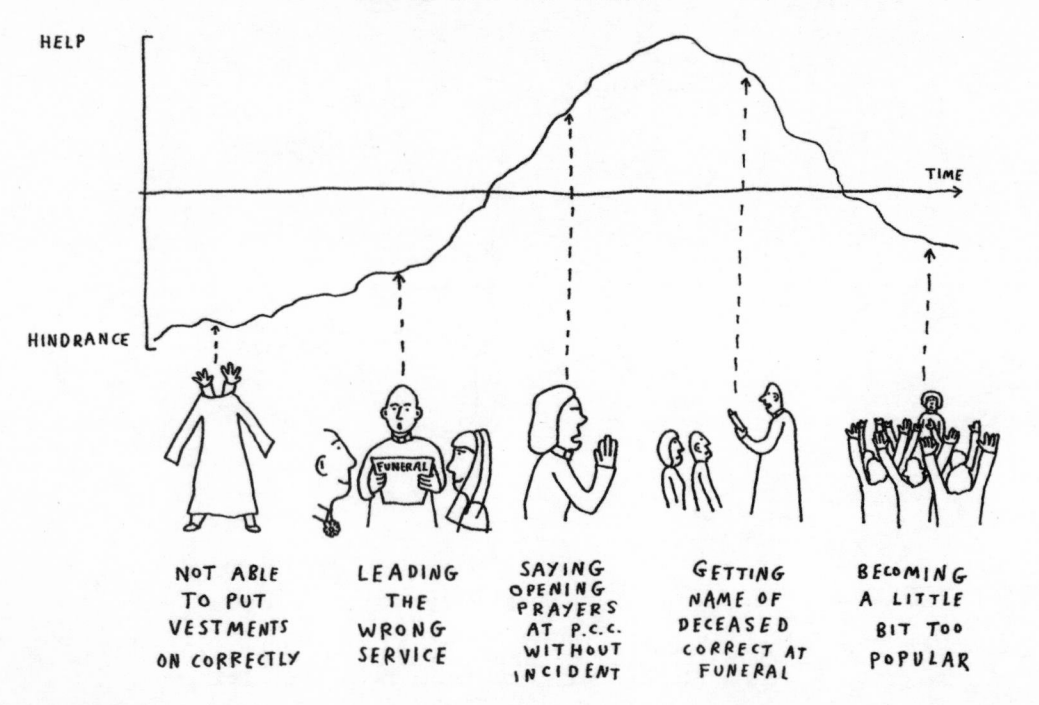

BAPTISM

SKILLS CLERGY REQUIRE

KNOWING HOW TO HOLD
THE BABY

DEALING WITH
UNFAMILIAR FONTS

EXCUSE ME...

MAKING SURE EVERYTHING
IS READY TO USE

FINDING THE CHILD
UNDER THE FRILLS

BIBLE
CANDLE
HYMN BOOK
ORDER OF SERVICE
BABY

HAVING ALL NECESSARY
ACCESSORIES TO HAND

PREVENTING INGESTION OF
THE RADIO MICROPHONE

CERTIFICATES

RECIPIENTS POSE WITH THEIR BISHOPS

COMPLETED LENT COURSE

TAUGHT SUNDAY SCHOOL

SURVIVED P.C.C.

ATTENDED SUNDAY SERVICE ON A NON-ROTA DAY

WEEKDAYS

WHAT TO DO WITH YOUR CHURCH BUILDING

LOCK IT

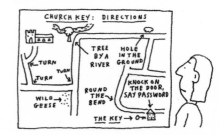

LEAVE A KEY SOMEWHERE

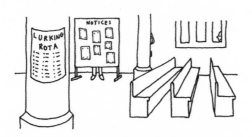

LEAVE IT OPEN, BUT MONITORED

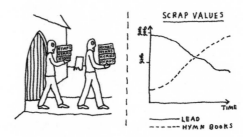

LEAVE IT ENTIRELY UNATTENDED

CHURCH CLEANING

HOW TO MAKE IT SEEM AS IF YOU HAVE DONE A GOOD JOB

SPRAY SOME POLISH IN THE AIR TO
GIVE THE REQUIRED AROMA

MAKE FULL USE OF LOOSE CARPETS

DO THE BITS THE VICAR CAN SEE

IF IN DOUBT: PUT IT IN THE VESTRY

CHURCH MAINTENANCE

A BASIC TOOL KIT

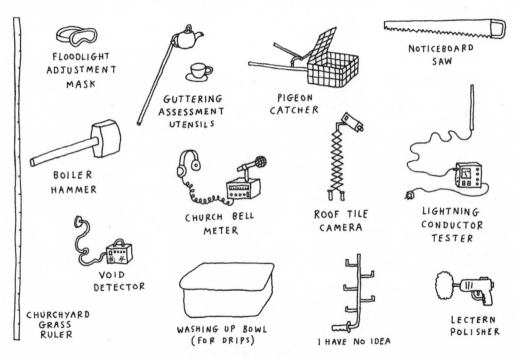

CHURCHYARD GRASS RULER

FLOODLIGHT ADJUSTMENT MASK

BOILER HAMMER

GUTTERING ASSESSMENT UTENSILS

PIGEON CATCHER

NOTICEBOARD SAW

CHURCH BELL METER

ROOF TILE CAMERA

LIGHTNING CONDUCTOR TESTER

VOID DETECTOR

WASHING UP BOWL (FOR DRIPS)

I HAVE NO IDEA

LECTERN POLISHER

TIDYING
ADVICE FOR CHURCH WORK PARTIES

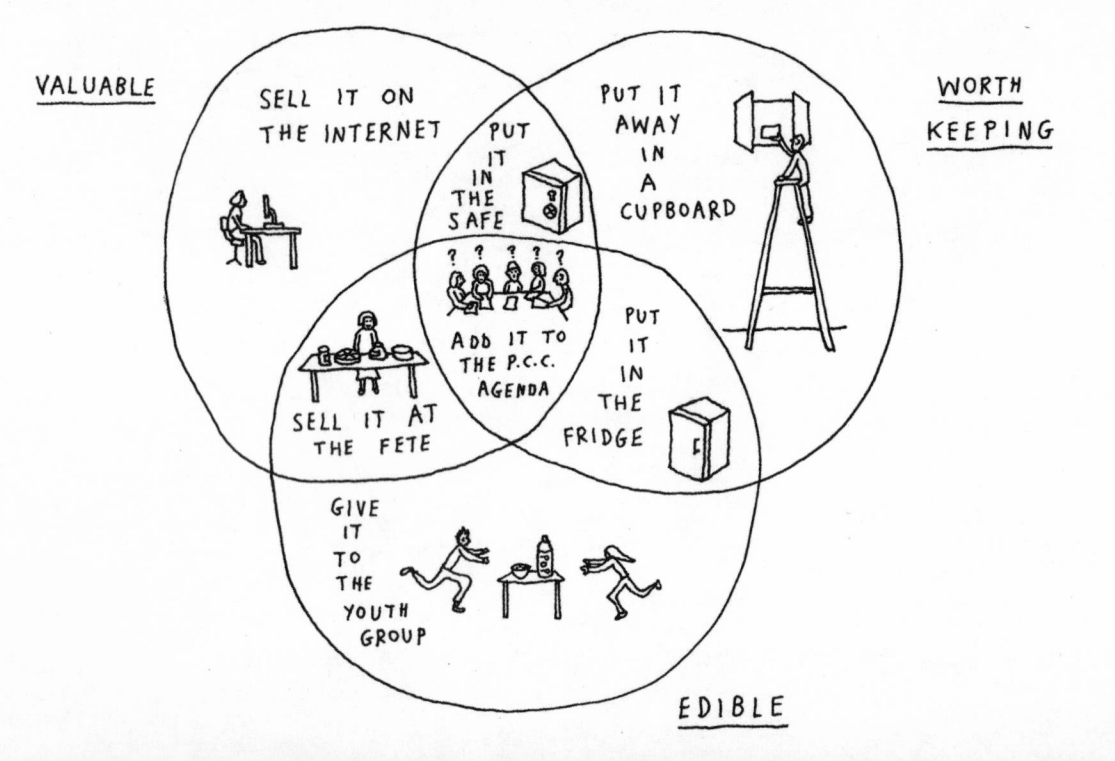

VALUABLE

WORTH KEEPING

SELL IT ON THE INTERNET

PUT IT IN THE SAFE

PUT IT AWAY IN A CUPBOARD

? ? ? ?
ADD IT TO THE P.C.C. AGENDA

SELL IT AT THE FETE

PUT IT IN THE FRIDGE

GIVE IT TO THE YOUTH GROUP

EDIBLE

TERRIBLE DISCOVERIES

THE BEAMS ARE ROTTEN AND COULD
COLLAPSE AT ANY MOMENT

OUR MOST PRECIOUS ARTEFACTS
HAVE BEEN STOLEN

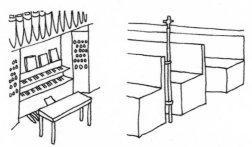

THE ORGANIST AND THE CHURCHWARDEN
HAVE GONE MISSING SIMULTANEOUSLY

SOMEONE HAS EATEN
ALL OF THE BISCUITS

ANIMALS

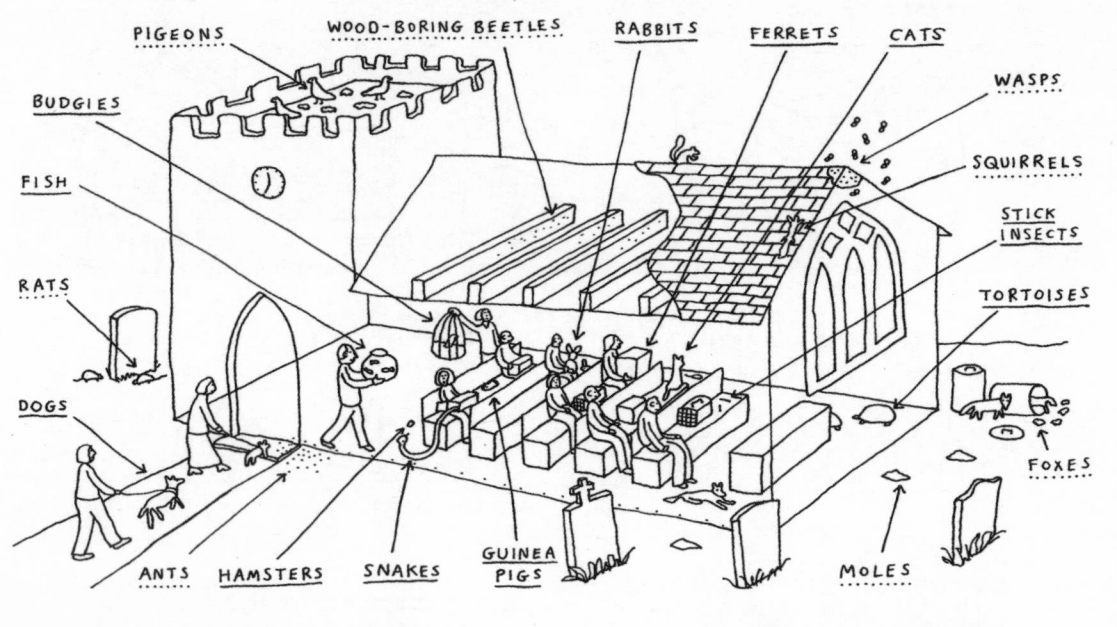

PIGEONS

WOOD-BORING BEETLES

RABBITS

FERRETS

CATS

WASPS

BUDGIES

SQUIRRELS

FISH

STICK INSECTS

RATS

TORTOISES

DOGS

FOXES

ANTS HAMSTERS SNAKES GUINEA PIGS MOLES

_____ THOSE WE HAVE INVITED
IN TO PARTICIPATE IN
OUR PET SERVICE

.... THOSE WE WOULD QUITE LIKE
TO BE ERADICATED BY THE
PEST-CONTROL PEOPLE

THE CHERRY PICKER

HOW TO USE IT

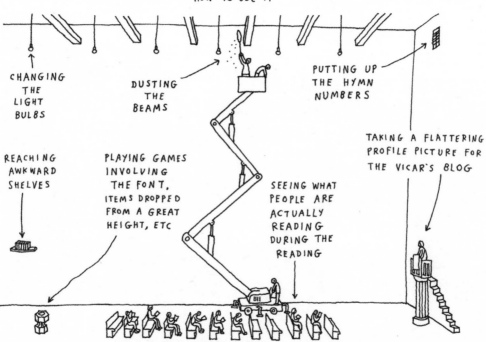

CHANGING THE LIGHT BULBS

DUSTING THE BEAMS

PUTTING UP THE HYMN NUMBERS

TAKING A FLATTERING PROFILE PICTURE FOR THE VICAR'S BLOG

REACHING AWKWARD SHELVES

PLAYING GAMES INVOLVING THE FONT, ITEMS DROPPED FROM A GREAT HEIGHT, ETC

SEEING WHAT PEOPLE ARE ACTUALLY READING DURING THE READING

THE CHURCH PORCH

PARENTS WITH CRYING CHILDREN

THOSE WALKING OUT OF SERMON ON THEOLOGICAL GROUNDS BUT PLANNING TO RETURN FOR COFFEE

RAMBLERS SEEKING SHELTER FROM THE RAIN

SMOKERS FROM THE BAPTISM PARTY

THE CHURCH PORCH IS A PLACE OF REFUGE

THE MOST IMPORTANT NOTICES ARE DISPLAYED

THE VICAR IS ALLOWED TO BORROW IT FOR GARDEN PARTIES

A PROPOSED UPVC REPLACEMENT HAS NOT PROVED VERY POPULAR

THE CHURCH TOWER

① ROOF AND FLAGPOLE

← WE SURRENDER

② THE CLOCK AND ITS MECHANISMS

REMEMBER: YOU **MUST** WIND IT THIS WAY*

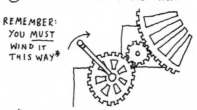

*AT LEAST I THINK SO. ASK MR LAWRENCE AT ROSE COTTAGE

③ THE SECRET CLERGY-TEAM CONTROL ROOM

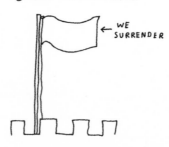

TARGETS

PARISH MAP

④ THE ROPES

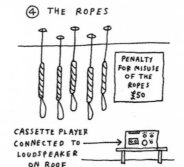

PENALTY FOR MISUSE OF THE ROPES £50

CASSETTE PLAYER CONNECTED TO LOUDSPEAKER ON ROOF →

CLEARING THE GUTTERS

ALL MANNER OF THINGS GATHER
IN THE CHURCH GUTTERS

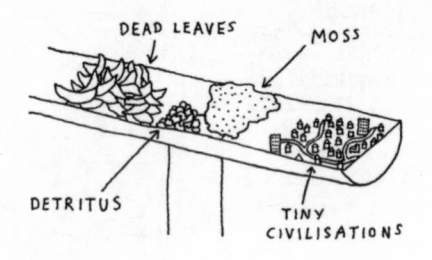

DEAD LEAVES

MOSS

DETRITUS

TINY
CIVILISATIONS

IF YOU DO NOT CLEAR THEM
YOU WILL HAVE PROBLEMS

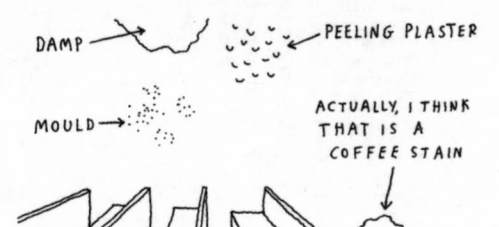

DAMP

PEELING PLASTER

MOULD →

ACTUALLY, I THINK
THAT IS A
COFFEE STAIN

THE TRADITIONAL SOLUTION: SEND
AN ELDERLY CHURCHWARDEN
UP A LADDER

ALTERNATIVELY YOU CAN
USE A LONG STICK.
A CROZIER IS IDEAL

MOST BISHOPS WON'T MIND
INCLUDING THIS SERVICE
WHEN THEY VISIT

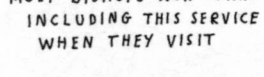

THE BINS

WHAT GOES WHERE

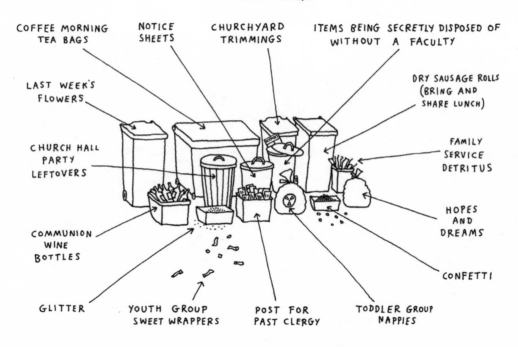

COFFEE MORNING TEA BAGS

NOTICE SHEETS

CHURCHYARD TRIMMINGS

ITEMS BEING SECRETLY DISPOSED OF WITHOUT A FACULTY

LAST WEEK'S FLOWERS

DRY SAUSAGE ROLLS (BRING AND SHARE LUNCH)

CHURCH HALL PARTY LEFTOVERS

FAMILY SERVICE DETRITUS

COMMUNION WINE BOTTLES

HOPES AND DREAMS

CONFETTI

GLITTER

YOUTH GROUP SWEET WRAPPERS

POST FOR PAST CLERGY

TODDLER GROUP NAPPIES

CHURCH CHAIRS

QUESTIONS TO ASK WHEN CHOOSING NEW ONES

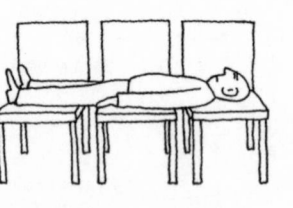

ARE THEY COMFORTABLE?

CAN THEY BE STACKED?

DO THEY SHOW THE DIRT?

CAN YOU HANG A
KNEELER ON THEM?

DO THEY LOOK APPROPRIATE?

WILL THE CONGREGATION
LIKE THEM?

REPAIRING THE HYMN BOOKS

THE CHURCH WEBSITE

WHO DID WHAT

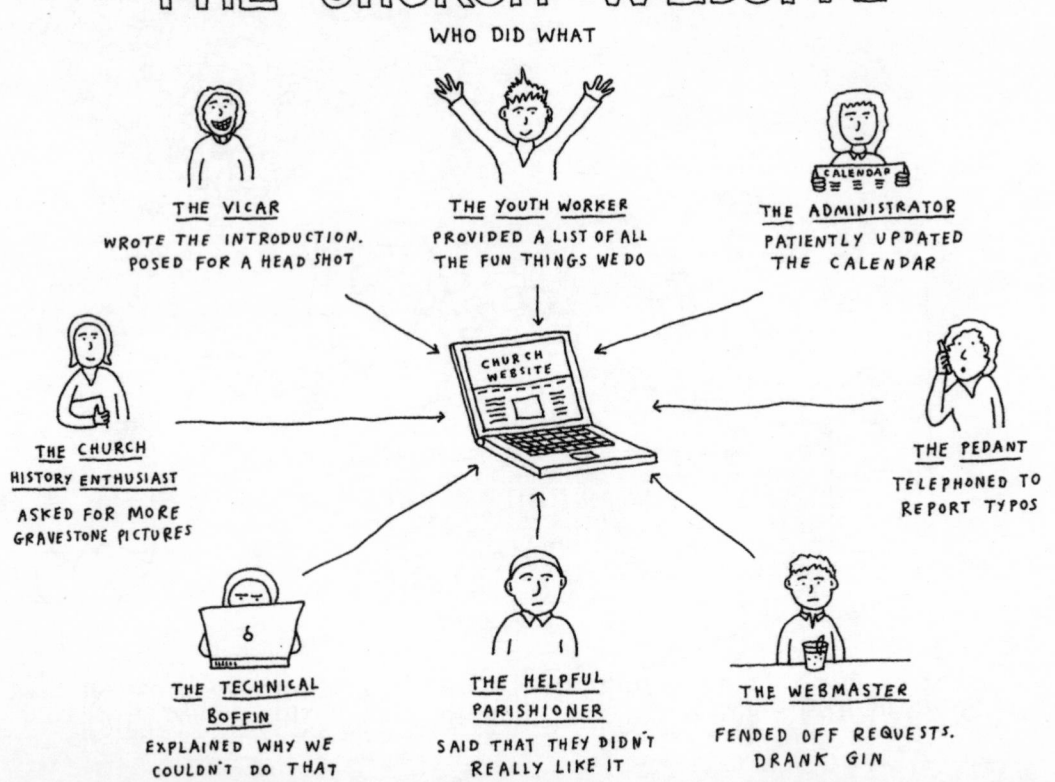

THE <u>VIC</u>AR
WROTE THE INTRODUCTION.
POSED FOR A HEAD SHOT

THE <u>YO</u>UTH WORKER
PROVIDED A LIST OF ALL
THE FUN THINGS WE DO

THE <u>ADMINISTRATO</u>R
PATIENTLY UPDATED
THE CALENDAR

THE <u>CHURC</u>H
<u>HISTORY ENTHUSIAS</u>T
ASKED FOR MORE
GRAVESTONE PICTURES

THE <u>PEDAN</u>T
TELEPHONED TO
REPORT TYPOS

THE <u>TECHNICAL</u>
BOFFIN
EXPLAINED WHY WE
COULDN'T DO THAT

THE <u>HELPFU</u>L
<u>PARISHIONE</u>R
SAID THAT THEY DIDN'T
REALLY LIKE IT

THE <u>WEBMASTE</u>R
FENDED OFF REQUESTS.
DRANK GIN

CYBER ATTACKS

HOW THE MODERN-DAY CHURCH IS RESISTING THEM

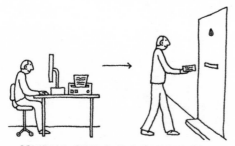

PRINTING EMAILS AND DELIVERING
THEM BY HAND

MAINTAINING ANTIVIRUS PROTECTION

KEEPING UP-TO-DATE INFORMATION
OFF THE WEBSITE

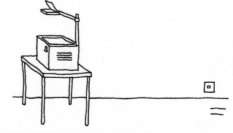

NOT PLUGGING THE OHP INTO THE INTERNET

AMPLIFICATION
METHODS USED

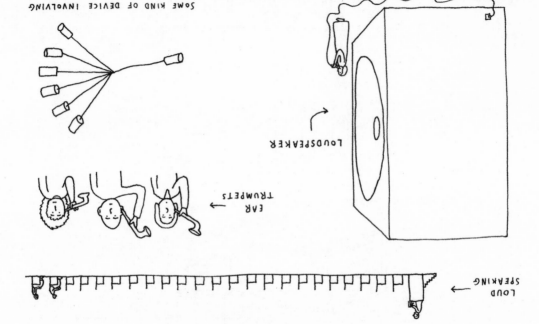

THE PERILS OF BEING TALL

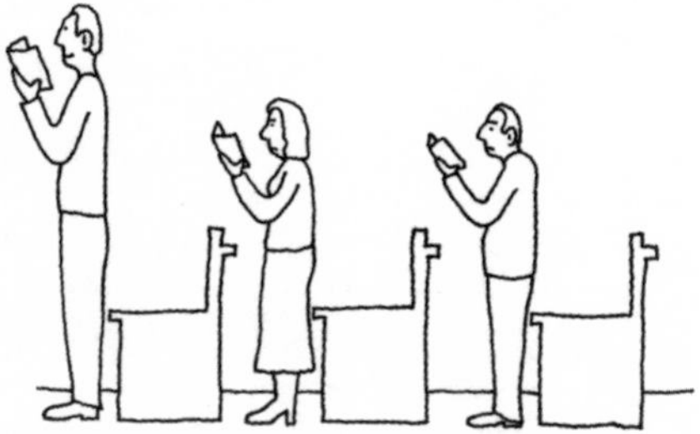

CAUSING AN OBSTRUCTION

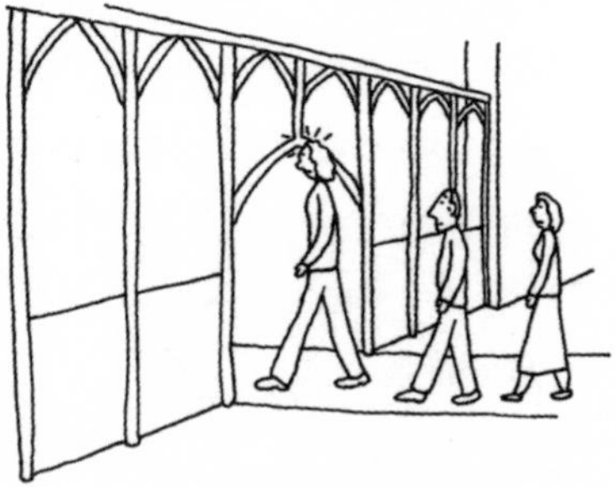

BANGING ONE'S HEAD

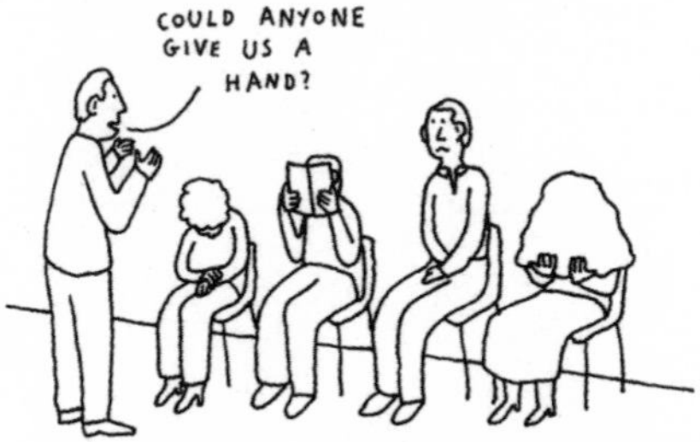
COULD ANYONE GIVE US A HAND?

IT IS DIFFICULT TO HIDE WHEN A VOLUNTEER IS REQUIRED

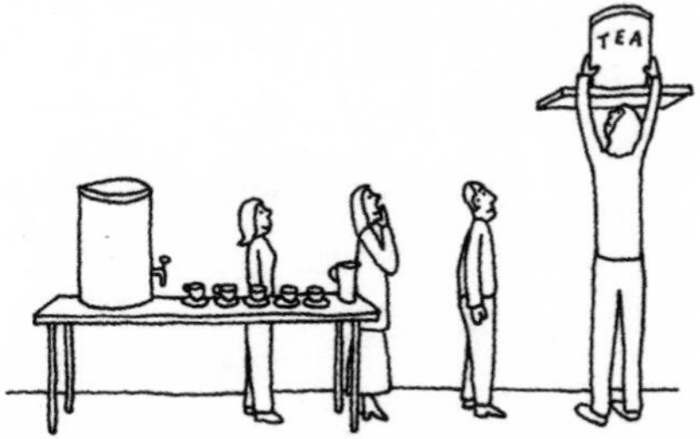
TEA

BEING ASKED TO RETRIEVE THINGS FROM HIGH SHELVES

LOST PROPERTY

THROUGH THE YEAR

Legend:

- 🌂 UMBRELLAS
- 🖐 GLOVES
- 🕶 SUNGLASSES
- 👓 READING GLASSES
- 🦵 ARTIFICIAL LIMBS
- 🧸 TOYS AND OTHER PARAPHERNALIA ASSOCIATED WITH CHILDREN
- 🎫 LOTTERY TICKET
- ✨ WINNING LOTTERY TICKET
- 🩱 SWIMWEAR
- 💭 HOPES AND DREAMS
- ⚬ MARBLES
- 🐎 PAPIER-MÂCHÉ ANIMALS
- 🦯 WALKING STICKS AND CRUTCHES
- 🧥 COATS
- 🍶 HIP FLASKS

ADVENT

WE LOOK FORWARD

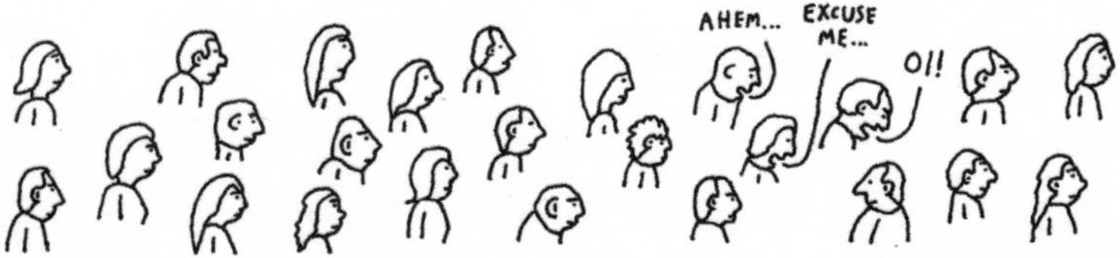

WE PREPARE

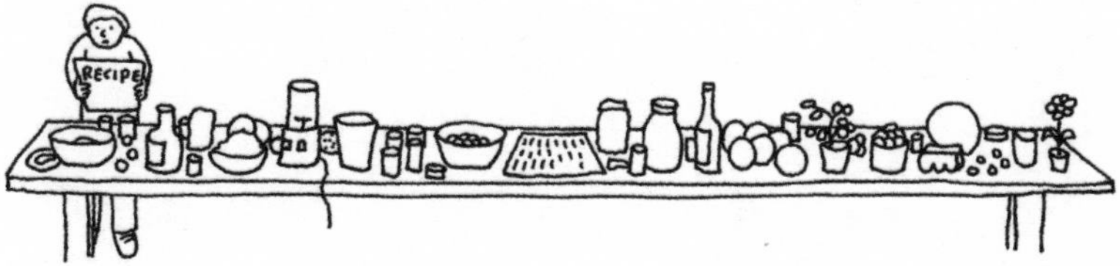

WE WAIT

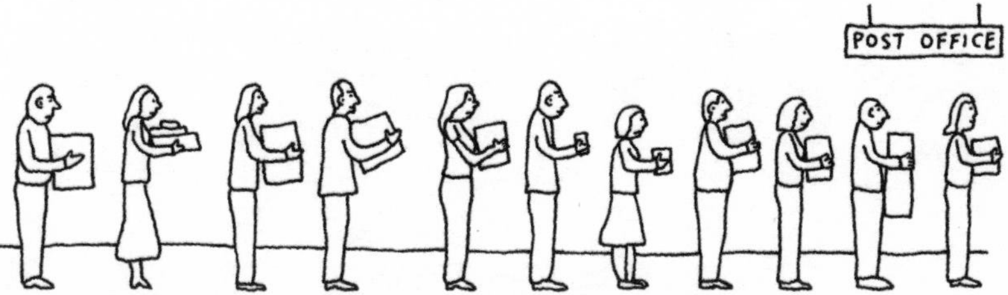

THE CHRISTMAS CHECKLIST

FOR CHURCHES

DIG OUT THE CRIB FIGURES ☐

DECORATE THE TREE AND CHURCH ☐

CHOOSE PEOPLE TO READ THE LESSONS ☐

MAKE SURE THE CHOIR IS READY ☐

DELIVER THE CHRISTMAS PUBLICITY LEAFLETS ☐

CLEAN EVERYWHERE ☐

DECIDE WHICH CLERGY DO WHICH SERVICES ☐

BUY PRESENTS FOR PEOPLE WHO HAVE WORKED HARD ☐

CARRY IN EXTRA CHAIRS ☐

REHEARSE THE NATIVITY PLAY ☐

WRITE ALL OF THE SERMONS ☐

PREPARE THE CANDLES ☐

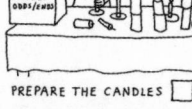

MAKE THE CHRISTINGLES ☐

COPY THE ORDERS OF SERVICE ☐

ORDER SUPPLIES FOR VICAR'S POST-CHRISTMAS BREAK ☐

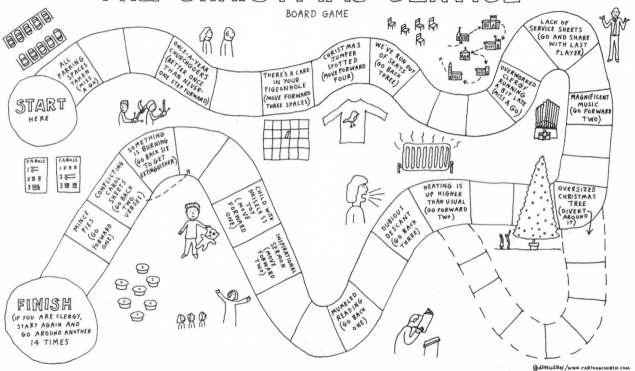

THE CHRISTMAS SERVICE
BOARD GAME

START HERE

ALL PARKING SPACES TAKEN (MISS A GO)

ONCE-A-YEAR CHURCHGOERS (BETTER ONCE THAN NEVER- ONE STEP FORWARD)

THERE'S A CARD IN YOUR PIGEONHOLE (MOVE FORWARD THREE SPACES)

CHRISTMAS JUMPER SPOTTED (MOVE FORWARD FOUR)

WE'VE RUN OUT OF SEATS (GO BACK THREE)

LACK OF SERVICE SHEETS (GO AND SHARE WITH LAST PLAYER)

OVERWORKED CLERGY RUNNING A BIT LATE (MISS A GO)

MAGNIFICENT MUSIC (GO FORWARD TWO)

OVERSIZED CHRISTMAS TREE (DIVERT AROUND IT)

HEATING IS UP HIGHER THAN USUAL (GO FORWARD TWO)

DUBIOUS DESCANT (GO BACK THREE)

MUMBLED READING (GO BACK ONE)

INSPIRATIONAL SERMON (MOVE FORWARD TWO)

CHILD WITH NOISELESS TOY (MOVE FORWARD ONE)

SOMETHING IS BURNING (GO BACK SIX TO GET EXTINGUISHER)

CONFLICTING CAROL SHEETS (GO BACK TWO VERSES)

MINCE PIES (GO FORWARD ONE)

CAROLS
1
2
3

CAROLS
1
2
3

FINISH (IF YOU ARE CLERGY, START AGAIN AND GO AROUND ANOTHER 14 TIMES)

@davewalker/www.cartoonchurch.com

WAYS TO KEEP WARM

IN CASE THERE IS ONE YOU HAVEN'T TRIED

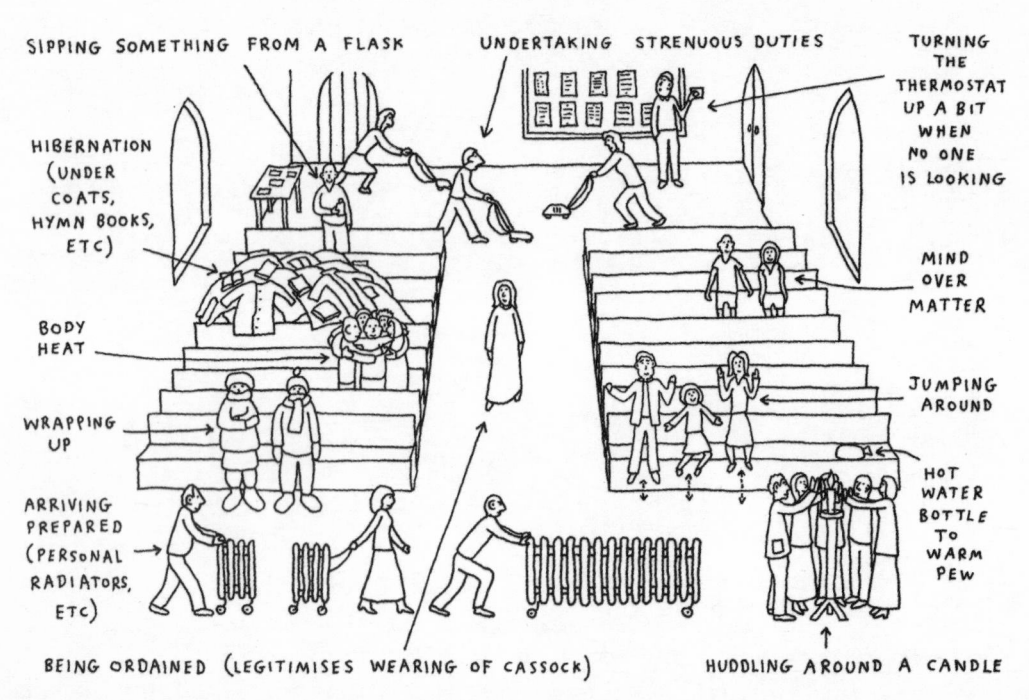

SIPPING SOMETHING FROM A FLASK

UNDERTAKING STRENUOUS DUTIES

TURNING THE THERMOSTAT UP A BIT WHEN NO ONE IS LOOKING

HIBERNATION (UNDER COATS, HYMN BOOKS, ETC)

MIND OVER MATTER

BODY HEAT

JUMPING AROUND

WRAPPING UP

HOT WATER BOTTLE TO WARM PEW

ARRIVING PREPARED (PERSONAL RADIATORS, ETC)

BEING ORDAINED (LEGITIMISES WEARING OF CASSOCK)

HUDDLING AROUND A CANDLE

THE EASTER FLOWERS

1. FORMULATING A VISION STATEMENT

2. MONTHS OF PLANNING AND DRINKING TEA

3. CHOOSING THE FLOWERS

4. CONSTRUCTION

THE FINISHED RESULT

BREAKING UP

HOW CHURCHES CELEBRATE THE END OF TERM

NON-UNIFORM DAY

PRIZEGIVING

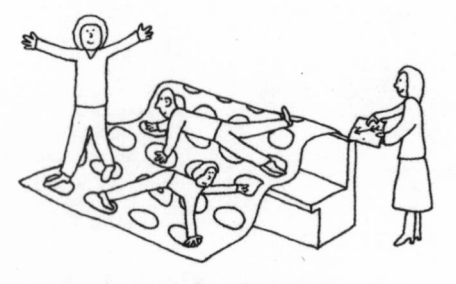

GAMES CAN BE BROUGHT IN

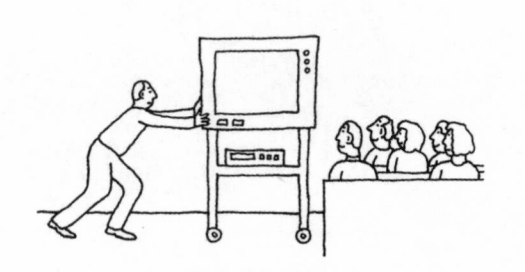

A VIDEO INSTEAD OF THE SERMON

THE HOLIDAY CLUB

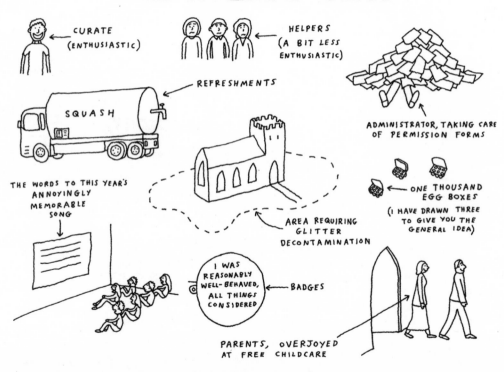

CURATE (ENTHUSIASTIC)

HELPERS (A BIT LESS ENTHUSIASTIC)

REFRESHMENTS

SQUASH

ADMINISTRATOR, TAKING CARE OF PERMISSION FORMS

THE WORDS TO THIS YEAR'S ANNOYINGLY MEMORABLE SONG

ONE THOUSAND EGG BOXES (I HAVE DRAWN THREE TO GIVE YOU THE GENERAL IDEA)

AREA REQUIRING GLITTER DECONTAMINATION

I WAS REASONABLY WELL-BEHAVED, ALL THINGS CONSIDERED

BADGES

PARENTS, OVERJOYED AT FREE CHILDCARE

THE EVOLUTION OF A FESTIVALGOER

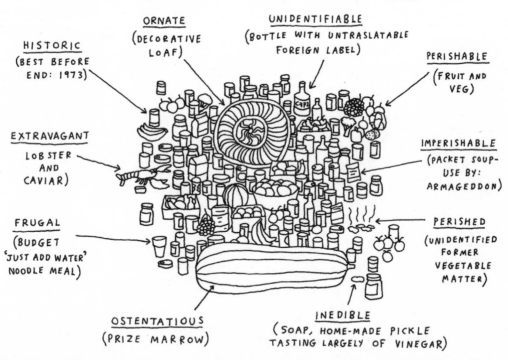

THE HARVEST FESTIVAL

THE GIFTS, ARRANGED IN THEIR VARIOUS CATEGORIES

HISTORIC
(BEST BEFORE
END: 1973)

ORNATE
(DECORATIVE
LOAF)

UNIDENTIFIABLE
(BOTTLE WITH UNTRASLATABLE
FOREIGN LABEL)

PERISHABLE
(FRUIT AND
VEG)

EXTRAVAGANT
LOBSTER
AND
CAVIAR)

IMPERISHABLE
(PACKET SOUP-
USE BY:
ARMAGEDDON)

FRUGAL
(BUDGET
'JUST ADD WATER'
NOODLE MEAL)

PERISHED
(UNIDENTIFIED
FORMER
VEGETABLE
MATTER)

OSTENTATIOUS
(PRIZE MARROW)

INEDIBLE
(SOAP, HOME-MADE PICKLE
TASTING LARGELY OF VINEGAR)

THE ART EXHIBITION

HIGHLIGHTS OF THIS YEAR'S DISPLAY, HELD IN THE CHURCH HALL AND CURATED BY THE CURATE

TRIPTYCH OF WORKS BY THE SUNDAY SCHOOL

"LEADING THE YOUTH GROUP" (BY THE YOUTH LEADER)

"SOME FLOWERS"

"UNTITLED (VERGER WITH KETTLE)"

"THE LAST 'BRING AND SHARE' SUPPER"

SMALL STATUETTE OF THE BISHOP (UNVEILED BY THE BISHOP)

"NUMBERS" (WORK SUBMITTED AT THE LAST MINUTE TO FILL SPACE)

PICTURES OF PREVIOUS VICARS WE WERE NOT ALLOWED TO TAKE DOWN

THE CATHEDRAL SHOP

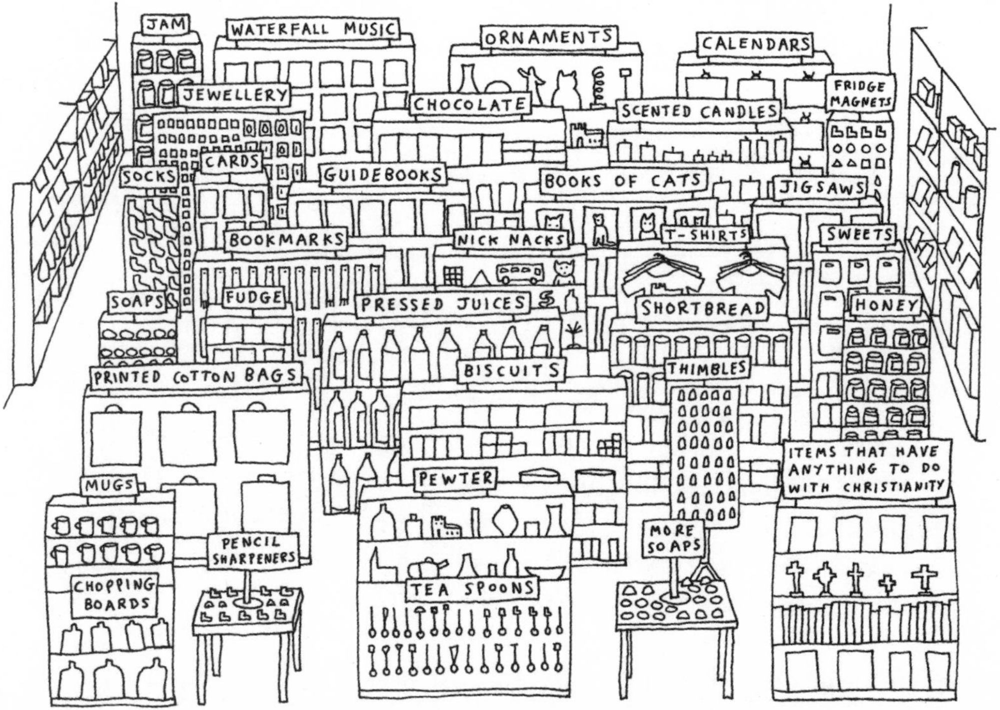
JAM
WATERFALL MUSIC
ORNAMENTS
CALENDARS
JEWELLERY
CHOCOLATE
SCENTED CANDLES
FRIDGE MAGNETS
CARDS
SOCKS
GUIDEBOOKS
BOOKS OF CATS
JIGSAWS
BOOKMARKS
NICK NACKS
T-SHIRTS
SWEETS
SOAPS
FUDGE
PRESSED JUICES
SHORTBREAD
HONEY
PRINTED COTTON BAGS
BISCUITS
THIMBLES
ITEMS THAT HAVE ANYTHING TO DO WITH CHRISTIANITY
MUGS
PEWTER
PENCIL SHARPENERS
MORE SOAPS
CHOPPING BOARDS
TEA SPOONS

THE SERMON ILLUSTRATION LENDING LIBRARY

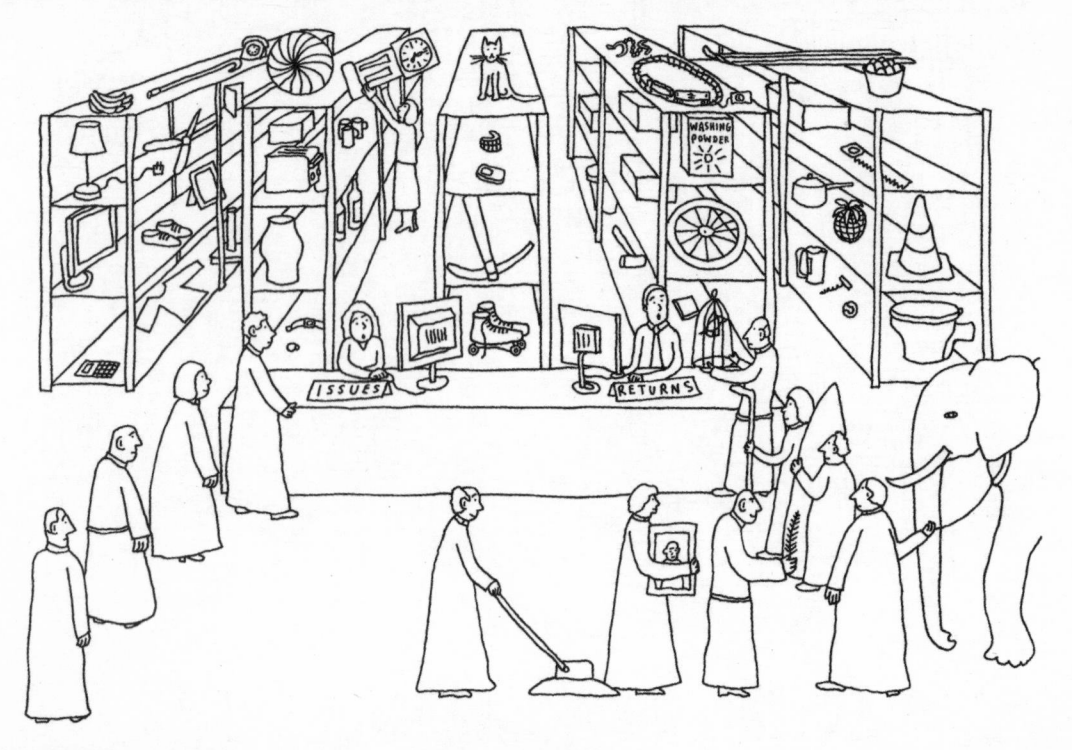

THE PILGRIMAGE

BEHAVIOUR EXHIBITED BY PARTICIPANTS

① SOUVENIR HUNTING (FINDING SHOP BEFORE CHURCH)

② PROSTRATION (IN FRONT OF ALTARS, ETC)

③ DUBIOUS MOTIVATION (ROMANTIC INTEREST IN GROUP LEADER)

④ CARRYING AN OLD TESTAMENT STAFF

⑤ CONFUSION (TOURIST WHO THINKS THIS IS A WALKING TOUR)

⑥ INAPPROPRIATE DRESS (NOT ALLOWED INTO HOLY SITES)

⑦ BUYING LOCAL CLOTHING (UNLIKELY TO BE WORN AGAIN)

⑧ WANDERING OFF

⑨ EVANGELISTIC FERVOUR

⑩ BIRD WATCHING (WHILE PRETENDING TO LOOK AT CHURCHES)

⑪ DISTRACTION (LOOKING AT THE WRONG THING)

⑫ ADDICTION (REALLY NEED A COFFEE SHOP)

WOMEN BISHOPS

WAYS OUT OF THIS MESS

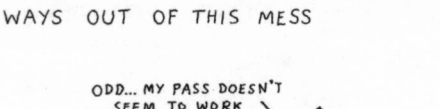

MAP OF DEBATING CHAMBER

LOCKED · LOCKED · LOCKED · TEA ROOM (CLOSED)

RECALL THE SYNOD SOON.
NO ONE LEAVES UNTIL
IT IS SORTED OUT

ODD... MY PASS DOESN'T SEEM TO WORK

HOUSE OF LORDS →

GET THE GOVERNMENT
TO DO SOMETHING

SAFETY HELMETS

INVENT A MACHINE TO
BANG TOGETHER THE HEADS
OF SYNOD MEMBERS

AND THE BISHOP LEAVING US TODAY IS... ... ...
... ...
VOTING LINES CLOSED

REFORM THE WAY THE
CHURCH MAKES DECISIONS

GOOD-LOOKING MEMBER OF CLERGY · SELF-PROMOTING BLOGGER · USUAL SUSPECT FROM MINORITY CHURCH GROUP

WORK IT OUT BY MEANS
OF TELEVISION DEBATES

OCCUPY THE BANKS

CHURCH GAMES

PART ONE

CHURCH HALL MOP

HASSOCK CURLING

5-A-SIDE
FLOWER ARRANGING

TOSSING THE
CROZIER

PASTORAL VISIT CYCLING

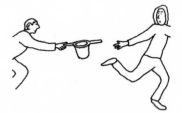

COLLECTION BAG
RELAY

100 METRES SPRINT
AWAY FROM THE ROTAS

CHURCH GAMES

PART TWO

PEW HURDLING

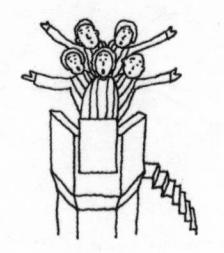

SYNCHRONISED PREACHING

BELL-RINGERS' TUG OF WAR

MARATHON CHURCH SERVICE

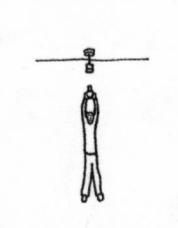

CHURCH MAINTENANCE
BY TRAMPOLINE

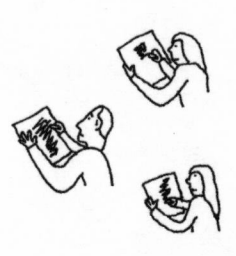

PRO-CELEBRITY BRASS RUBBING

THE SMOKE STACK

UNDERSTANDING THE SIGNALS FROM THE CHURCH KITCHEN CHIMNEY

BLACK

SOMEONE HAS INTERFERED
WITH THE TOASTER SETTINGS

WHITE

WE ARE BURNING INCRIMINATING
P.C.C. MINUTES

STEAM

UNATTENDED
URN

NOTHING

THE BOILER HAS BROKEN
DOWN AGAIN

FLAMES

OH DEAR

MOP

OVERENTHUSIASM AT THE
CHURCH WORK PARTY DAY

THE NEW ARCHBISHOP

IMPORTANT TASKS FOR THE FIRST WEEK

GET MEASURED FOR NEW KIT

FIND OUT WHERE THINGS ARE

DECIDE UPON A SIGNATURE

ARRANGE DESK

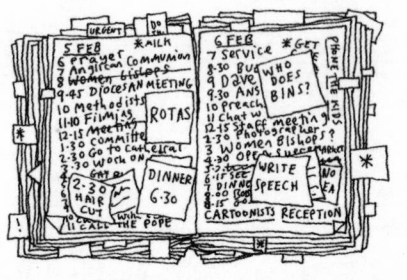

TAKE A LOOK AT THE APPOINTMENTS DIARY

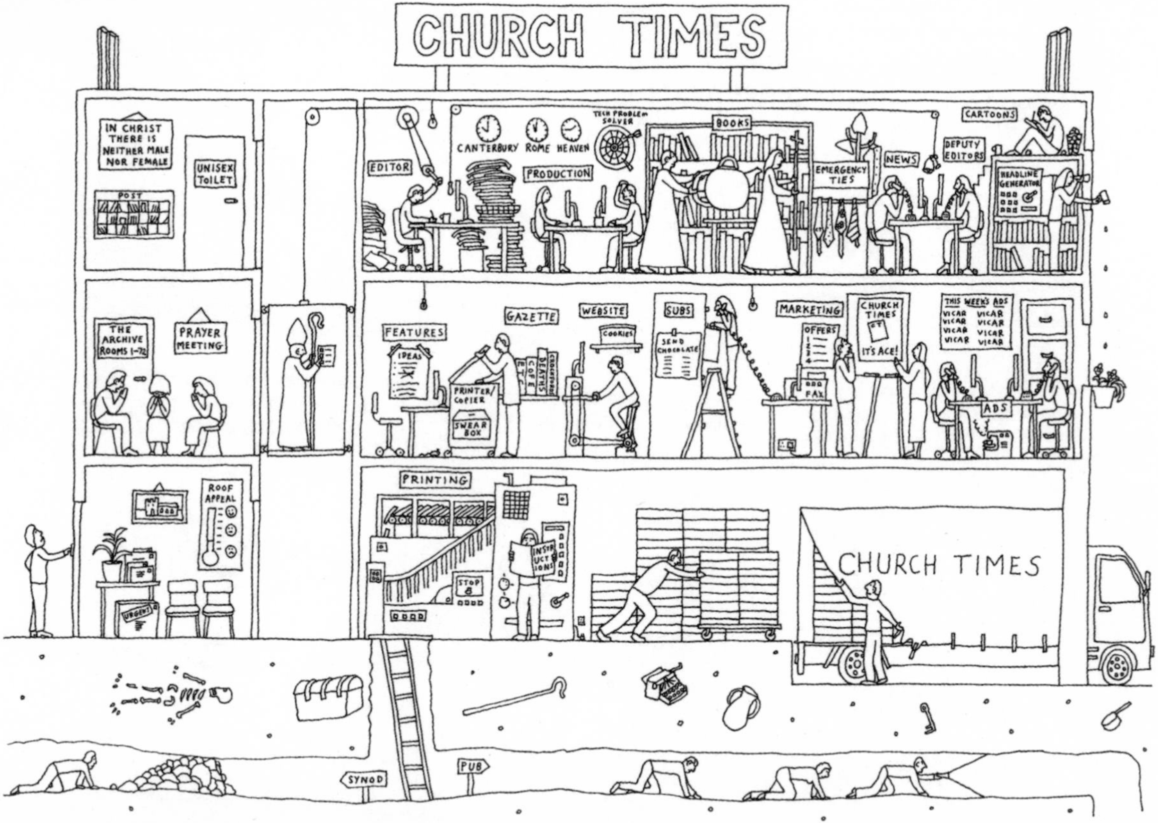
CHURCH TIMES
IN CHRIST THERE IS NEITHER MALE NOR FEMALE
UNISEX TOILET
POST
EDITOR
CANTERBURY ROME HEAVEN
TECH PROBLEM SOLVER
PRODUCTION
BOOKS
EMERGENCY TIES
NEWS
DEPUTY EDITORS
CARTOONS
HEADLINE GENERATOR
THE ARCHIVE ROOMS 1–72
PRAYER MEETING
FEATURES
IDEAS
GAZETTE
DEATHS
C of E
CROCKFORDS
PRINTER/COPIER
SWEAR BOX
WEBSITE
COOKIES
SUBS
SEND CHOCOLATE
MARKETING
OFFERS
CHURCH TIMES
CT
IT'S ACE!
FAX
THIS WEEK'S ADS
VICAR VICAR
VICAR VICAR
VICAR VICAR
VICAR VICAR
ADS
ROOF APPEAL
URGENT
PRINTING
STOP
INSTRUCTIONS
CHURCH TIMES
SYNOD
PUB

THE LITERARY FESTIVAL

AUTHORS SIGNING BOOKS FOR
PEOPLE WHOSE NAMES THEY OUGHT
TO KNOW BUT HAVE FORGOTTEN

WRITERS PRETENDING NOT TO
BE INTERESTED IN BOOK AWARDS

AUTHORS REORGANISING
COPIES OF THEIR BOOKS
IN THE BOOKSHOP

AUDIENCE MEMBERS USING
QUESTION TIMES TO SHARE
THEIR VIEWS AT GREAT LENGTH

GHOST WRITERS

PRIORITIES DURING THE
MID-MORNING BREAK

THE FOODBANK

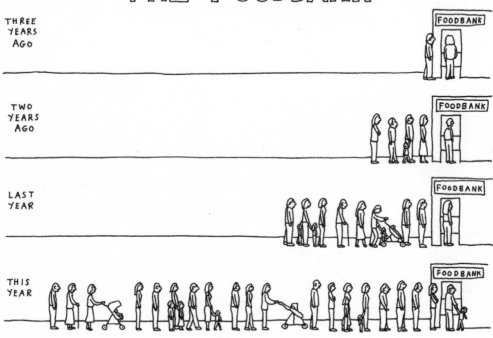

THREE YEARS AGO

TWO YEARS AGO

LAST YEAR

THIS YEAR

PERHAPS WE NEED TO ASK WHY THIS IS HAPPENING

PERPETUAL ECONOMIC GROWTH

DEMONSTRATED USING...

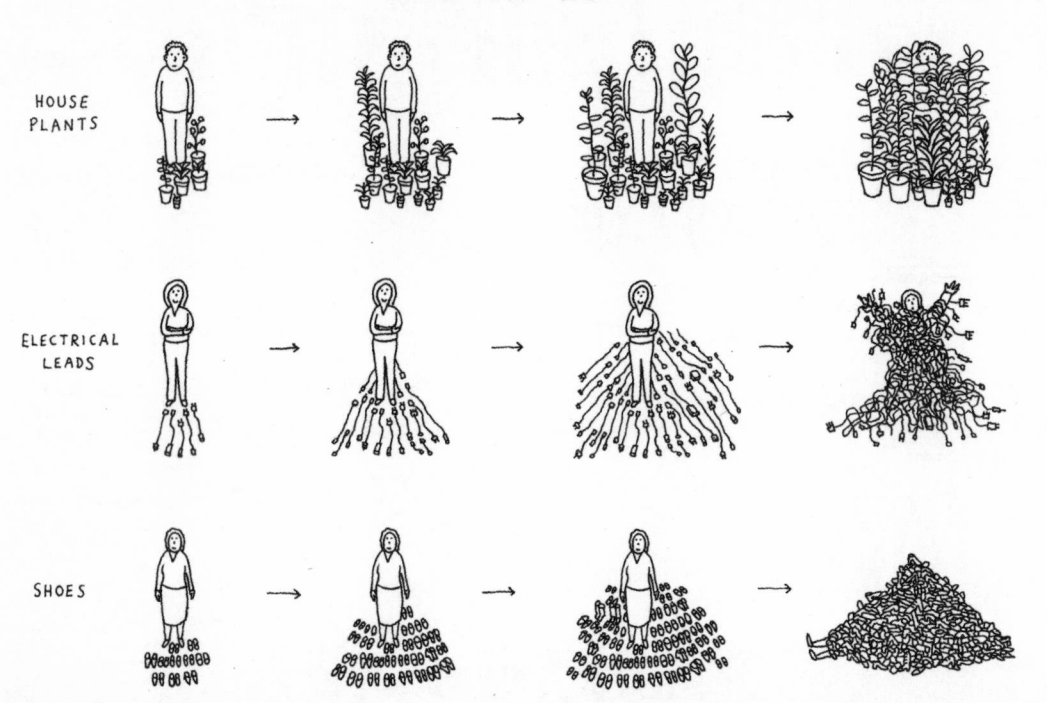

HOUSE PLANTS

ELECTRICAL LEADS

SHOES

EXECUTIVE PAY

DIAGRAM EXPLAINING WHY SENIOR EXECUTIVES DESERVE TO BE PAID
ONE HUNDRED TIMES AS MUCH AS THE REGULAR EMPLOYEES

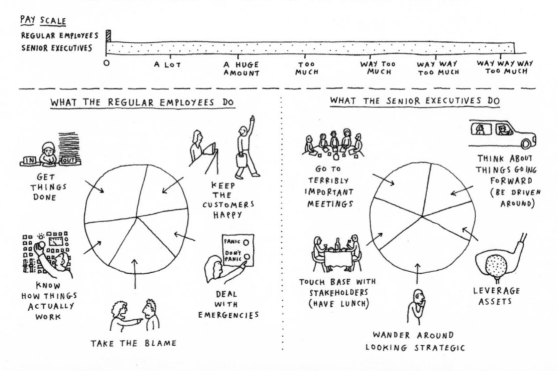

PAY SCALE

REGULAR EMPLOYEES
SENIOR EXECUTIVES

O · A LOT · A HUGE AMOUNT · TOO MUCH · WAY TOO MUCH · WAY WAY TOO MUCH · WAY WAY WAY TOO MUCH

WHAT THE REGULAR EMPLOYEES DO

GET THINGS DONE

KEEP THE CUSTOMERS HAPPY

KNOW HOW THINGS ACTUALLY WORK

PANIC ○
DON'T PANIC ○

DEAL WITH EMERGENCIES

TAKE THE BLAME

WHAT THE SENIOR EXECUTIVES DO

GO TO TERRIBLY IMPORTANT MEETINGS

THINK ABOUT THINGS GOING FORWARD (BE DRIVEN AROUND)

TOUCH BASE WITH STAKEHOLDERS (HAVE LUNCH)

LEVERAGE ASSETS

WANDER AROUND LOOKING STRATEGIC

TIME TO CHOOSE

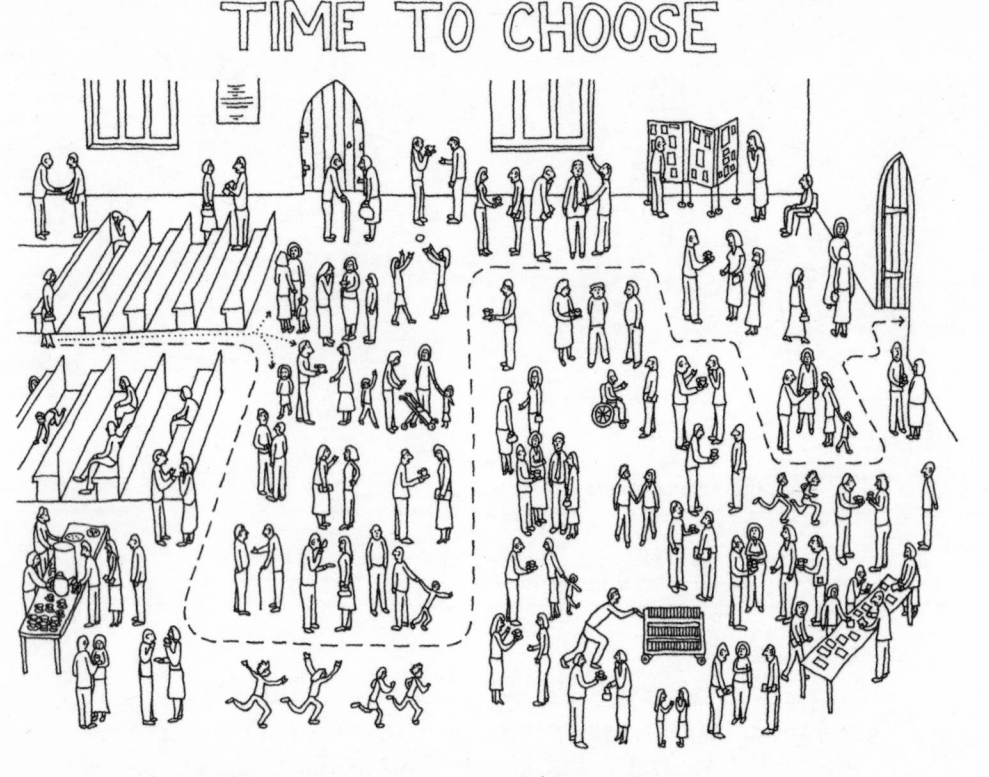

1) CONVERSATION ······················>   2) ESCAPE – – – – – →